The Radiance of God

The Radiance of God

Christian Doctrine through the Image of Divine Light

Douglas M. Koskela

CASCADE *Books* · Eugene, Oregon

THE RADIANCE OF GOD
Christian Doctrine through the Image of Divine Light

Cascade Books
An Imprint of Wipf and Stock Publishers
199 W. 8th Ave., Suite 3
Eugene, OR 97401

www.wipfandstock.com

PAPERBACK ISBN: 978-1-7252-6107-5
HARDCOVER ISBN: 978-1-7252-6108-2
EBOOK ISBN: 978-1-7252-6109-9

Cataloguing-in-Publication data:

Names: Koskela, Douglas M., 1972–, author
Title: The radiance of God : Christian doctrine through the image of divine light / Douglas M. Koskela.
Description: Eugene, OR: Cascade Books, 2021 | Includes bibliographical references.
Identifiers: ISBN 978-1-7252-6107-5 (paperback) | ISBN 978-1-7252-6108-2 (hardcover) | ISBN 978-1-7252-6109-9 (ebook)
Subjects: LCSH: Light—Religious aspects—Christianity | Theology, Doctrinal
Classification: BT65 K67 2021 (print) | BT65 (ebook)

For Nathan and Ally

Table of Contents

Acknowledgments

I WISH TO EXPRESS my gratitude to the many people who have supported this project in various ways as it took shape. As always, my colleagues in the School of Theology at Seattle Pacific University have provided immeasurable encouragement, guidance, and technical expertise. In particular, conversations with Daniel Castelo, Sara Koenig, Mike Langford, Bo Lim, Matt Sigler, Frank Spina, Rick Steele, Doug Strong, and Rob Wall have helped me greatly along the way. I am also thankful for the interest my students have taken in this project and for the feedback they have offered at various points.

Special thanks are due to Jason Vickers, editor of the *Wesleyan Theological Journal*, for permission to use some material from an article that I published there previously.

I would also like to extend my appreciation to the team at Wipf and Stock/Cascade, who have been wonderful partners in seeing this book through to publication. Michael Thomson, once again, grasped the vision of this book immediately and supported its development, particularly in the early stages.

Finally, my family has been a source of encouragement, companionship, and joy during the writing process. I am very thankful to my wife Jamie and my kids, Nathan and Ally, for taking an interest in what I was writing and for always being willing to talk with me about it. I give thanks to God for the light that is reflected in their lives.

Introduction

"GOD IS LIGHT," WE read in 1 John 1:5, "and in him there is no darkness at all." Given the darkness that we all experience in the world, that proclamation comes as good news indeed. Just a glimpse of the divine radiance shining amidst the darkness is sufficient to bring hope. Such a sight suggests not only that the current night will pass, but also that the day to come will bring a joy as yet unimagined for those who welcome it. This is the effect of God's self-revelation coming into a broken and suffering world, and it is at the heart of Christian proclamation. That revelation—and thus, our proclamation—is centered in the person of Jesus, the light of the world.

To behold the light of God, in such ways as we are able in this life, is to be drawn toward God. In that movement, we do not remain the same. We are transformed into the likeness of what we have seen. The apostle Paul put the point this way in 2 Corinthians 3:18: "And all of us, with unveiled faces, seeing the glory of the Lord as though reflected in a mirror, are being transformed into the same image from one degree of glory to another; for this comes from the Lord, the Spirit." The Holy Spirit's transformative work moves us closer to the divine light and graciously prepares us to share in it. In a passage from the Homilies of Pseudo-Macarius, we find a striking portrait of union between the beholder and that which is beheld: "For the soul that is deemed to be judged worthy to participate in the light of the Holy Spirit by becoming his throne and habitation, and is covered with the beauty of ineffable glory of the Spirit, becomes all light, all face, all eye. There is no part of the soul that is not full of the spiritual eyes of light."[1] This transformation brings us fully into the purpose for which we were created: to love, worship, and delight in the triune God.

This book is an exploration of Christian doctrine through the lens of one particular image, that of divine light. Its thesis can be stated quite

---

1. Pseudo-Macarius, *Homilies*, 1.2 (p. 37 in the Maloney translation).

simply. The image of God as light enables the articulation of the Christian gospel in terms of three central concepts: allure, movement, and joy. I have in mind here the most basic meaning of the term "gospel"; namely, the very good news that we noted at the outset. The activity of the triune God in history is both revelatory and salvific, and the consequence of that activity comes as good news to all who will receive it. As we explore this gospel from the angle of the divine radiance, we will walk through the various loci of Christian doctrine. There is a natural connection between the gospel and basic Christian teaching. As the good news was proclaimed from the apostolic era on, various intellectual and practical questions arose. The central Christian doctrines about God, creation, salvation, and the like emerged as the church reflected prayerfully on Scripture, under the guidance of the Holy Spirit, in response to these questions. This body of teaching about God's nature and work, grounded in divine revelation, provides the intellectual framework in which the gospel makes sense.

It should go without saying that we will not be able to undertake a comprehensive account of Christian doctrine in what follows. When one particular angle of vision is used—in this case, the divine light—it is simply not possible to address every contour of Christian teaching. Yet it is hoped that what is given up in comprehensiveness will be gained in coherence. The imagery of light and darkness enables a focused expression of the gospel across the range of doctrine. Our approach will center on the recurring themes of allure, movement, and joy. The three main sections of each chapter will take up these concepts with an eye to the area of doctrine under consideration.

By *allure*, we are referring to the beauty of the divine light. To glimpse God's radiance is to be captivated by its brilliance. The light draws our attention from the darkness of our present circumstances to the source of that light. In the first progression of each chapter, then, we will consider the attraction of the divine radiance that initiates our movement toward God. *Movement* refers to the transformation that occurs as we progress from darkness to light. This is properly the work of the Holy Spirit, as we are formed in the likeness of Christ and prepared to share in the divine light eternally. We will explore the dynamics of this movement in the second section of each chapter, in ways appropriate to the respective doctrinal loci. Finally, the theme of *joy* expresses the experience of basking in the radiance of God. While we enjoy a sense of this bliss throughout the journey toward union with God, the culmination of that journey will involve the unfiltered joy of participation in the divine light. Therefore, the third progression of each chapter will be focused on the end to which our transformation is directed.

As we take this approach throughout the book, we will often find that we explore the same terrain from multiple points of entry. For example, the section on movement in each chapter considers the transformative import of the divine-human encounter. But the specific doctrine at the core of a given chapter will determine the direction from which we explore that encounter. In that respect, one might think of the form of the discussion as a sort of spiral that continually revisits our three themes as we walk through the classic Christian doctrines. Again, the goal is to tell a coherent story of good news: that "the light shines in the darkness, and the darkness did not overcome it" (John 1:5).

Given the prominence of the image of light in the Christian tradition, and particularly in Orthodoxy, a few disclaimers are in order. First, in this discussion I am taking radiance primarily as an image of God's glory. Thus it is compatible with, but not committed to, particular metaphysical accounts of the uncreated divine light such as one finds in the Eastern Orthodox tradition. Second, we need to distinguish from the outset the allure-movement-joy triad from the purification-illumination-union triad that we find in a variety of figures, perhaps most prominently in Pseudo-Dionysius. While readers may detect some overlap at a number of points, the orientation of our triad is rather different. One key difference is that the category of allure begins earlier, both logically and temporally, in the spiritual journey than the category of purification. To consider the allure of the divine radiance, we are asking what draws one into the journey toward the light. Another difference is that the categories of purification and illumination would both fall more or less under the heading of movement in our schema. There are other distinctions we could draw, but it suffices to say at this stage that our three categories are not simply new terms for these classical categories. Finally, while we will occasionally encounter the common use of light imagery to signify a particular sort of knowledge from God, that is not the primary emphasis. There is no doubt that an encounter with the divine radiance has epistemological consequences, which we will explore in some detail in chapters 5 and 6. But our primary interest is in light as an image of the glory of God.

It is perhaps clear by now that the discussion that follows is not an exhaustive historical or exegetical treatment of the concept of divine light.

The goal is not to trace how the image of light has been used by various figures in the Christian tradition. Rather, the task is primarily dogmatic and constructive. We aim to draw on the resources of the tradition to articulate the good news of the Christian faith through the lens of divine radiance. Readers may notice that the posture in which the book is written shares a great deal in common with premodern approaches to theological discourse. I proceed primarily by reading Scripture over the shoulders of those who have come before us in the faith. I write as a confessing Christian, shaped by the ecumenical riches of the church catholic and particularly by my own Wesleyan tradition. While there is inevitably a descriptive component involved as we try to get clear on what various texts actually say, the primary modes of discourse are testimony and worship. I am trying to point to, and give thanks for, the light of God that has given hope to people walking in darkness throughout the centuries. Toward that end, we will encounter the voices of those who have been transformed by that light and have tried to lead us toward it. My ultimate hope is that my deep love for the radiant God will come through in these pages. That love, which flows entirely from the love God has for us all (1 John 4:19), has motivated all that follows.

1

God the Father

"His Radiance Is Like the Sunlight"

WHEN ONE STEPS INTO the world of theology, a problem emerges quickly and sharply: what does one say? How does one dare to speak of the transcendent God in a way that gets us closer to the truth? This is perhaps the fundamental theological problem, and the Christian tradition is not without many helpful points of guidance. One bedrock guideline is to remain close to what God has revealed about Godself. If the very possibility of speaking truthfully about God only arises because of God's self-disclosure, then that disclosure must shape theological speech at every turn. Another guideline is to keep in mind that theology makes regular use of a mode of discourse known as analogical predication. That is, the ways we use language when speaking of God are both like and unlike the ways we use that same language in everyday conversation. Many theologians would suggest that this applies not only to images we use to talk about God—like a rock or a shepherd—but also to attributes like goodness and justice.[1] Suffice it to say that when we are using obvious images to say something about God, it is clear that those images are both like and unlike the divine reality to which they point.

These two principles—and there are certainly more, but these two hold us on course at present—lead us naturally to the image of light. As we will see, to speak of God in terms of radiance is to attend to an image that is used extensively in Scripture and the Christian tradition. And, true

---

1. See, for example, Aquinas, *Summa Theologiae*, I.13.5–10.

to analogues in general, light is both *like* and *unlike* the God to whom it points. The usefulness of this image has been recognized in the tradition because there are so many points of likeness: light suggests glory, draws our attention, enables vision, brings hope, reveals truth, and symbolizes joy. And yet precisely because of the power of this image, we must keep in mind that the reality of God transcends what any image is able to capture. Irenaeus perhaps overstates this point when he writes: "He may most correctly be called Light, but He is nothing like our light."[2] Our experience with light can point us in a helpful direction, but only when we keep its discontinuities with the divine reality firmly in mind.

A couple of interesting puzzles emerge when we turn our attention to this image. One arises when we try to identify the referent of the claim that God is light: is it the Father, the Son, the Spirit, or the Trinity as a whole? A second puzzle is that language of both light and darkness appears in the Christian tradition in reference to God. How can we make sense of the material on darkness, given our guiding image of God as light? We will explore both of these questions in this chapter. As is the case in each chapter of the book, our discussion will proceed in three main progressions: allure, movement, and joy. In the section on allure, we will explore the sheer attractiveness of God as light. Along the way, we will take up the question posed by our first puzzle above. Our exploration of movement will consider the transformative effect of an encounter with the radiant God on God's creatures. In that section, we will examine the place of the theme of darkness raised in our second puzzle. Finally, our account of joy will focus on the culmination of that encounter; namely, the blessing of knowing God as light.

Allure: Drawn to the Radiant Glory

One of the more vivid biblical instances of the image of divine light is found in Isaiah 60. At the beginning of that passage, the city of Jerusalem is addressed as the locus of God's radiance: "Arise, shine; for your light has come, and the glory of the LORD has risen upon you. For darkness shall cover the earth, and thick darkness the peoples; but the LORD will arise upon you, and his glory will appear over you. Nations shall come to your light, and kings to the brightness of your dawn" (v. 1–3). The brilliance of God's glory

2. Irenaeus, *Against Heresies* II.13.4 (vol. 2, p. 43 of the Unger translation). Augustine makes a similar point in *Confessions*, X.vi.8.

shining over the holy city is so attractive in this vision that even the nations and their kings are drawn to it. And the appeal of that radiance is not mere spectacle; the very promise of salvation is implied in this vision of light. As Arthur Michael Ramsey suggests in his classic treatment of the glory of God, the post-exilic vision of the last part of Isaiah brought together God's attributes, God's salvific action, and God's sheer appeal: "Indeed, in the *kabod* [glory] of Yahveh radiance, power, and righteous character are inextricably blended; and the word thus tells of a theology in which the attributes of God in Himself are inseparable from His attractiveness and saving activity in the world."[3] The God who saves is not a mere warrior; rather, God is a source of light and an object of beauty to behold.

Beyond its immediate historical context, the Isaiah 60 passage points to an enduring feature of the image of light: its sheer attraction. In a state of darkness, recognized or unrecognized, we are drawn to light as a source of hope and joy. It is thus natural for God's people to turn to this image to articulate their experience of delight in encountering God in the midst of darkness. But given its use in explicitly Christian theology, just what or whom are we seeing when we behold this light? That is, how can we think through this image in *trinitarian* terms? There is, to be sure, plenty of biblical support for the idea that the image is best focused on the person of the Son. In chapter 3, we will explore these texts—and the particular importance of the Johannine material to this end. There are also good reasons for thinking first and foremost of the person of the Holy Spirit, not least of which is the prominent place that illumination holds among the works of the Spirit. We will consider more along these lines in chapter 5.

But what about God the Father? On the one hand, Christians have understandably been hesitant to speak of the direct perception of God the Father. The recognition of the incapacity of finite creatures to see the transcendent God is reflected in Israel's faith practices, perhaps best crystallized in the commandment against graven images. Caution about depicting God the Father in Christian iconography—rooted largely in the care with which the Seventh Ecumenical Council expressed the christological basis of iconography—is an echo of the same instinct. The most direct access we have to apprehension of God the Father is through the Son's incarnation in Jesus. One thinks immediately, for example, of Jesus's reply to Philip in John 14:9: "Whoever has seen me has seen the Father." On the other hand, that very claim, grounded in Jesus's insistence that "the Father is in me"

3. Ramsey, *The Glory of God*, 14.

(v. 10), suggests that the Father is not entirely hidden from our perception. The incarnate Son is not to be thought of as a mask that covers the true face of the Father, but rather the Son reflects the likeness of the Father as one in whom the Father dwells. When we use the image of God as light, then, does it not follow that the light is in some sense the light of God the Father?

Voices in the tradition have answered clearly in the affirmative, making use of two primary moves. The first is to orient the image of light with reference to the Triune God, with the Father as the source of the light. We see an example of this in Gregory of Nazianzus's Fifth Theological Oration. His immediate purpose is to defend the full divinity of the Holy Spirit, and he does so by appealing to the shared light of the Trinity:

> "He was the true light that enlightens every man coming into the world"—yes, the Father. "He was the true light that enlightens every man coming into the world"—yes, the Son. "He was the true light that enlightens every man coming into the world"—yes, the Comforter. These are three subjects and three verbs—he was and he was and he was. But a single reality *was*. There are three predicates—light and light and light. But the light is one, God is one. This is the meaning of David's prophetic vision: "In your light we shall see light." We receive the Son's light from the Father's light in the light of the Spirit.[4]

Gregory here echoes Psalm 36:9 ("in your light shall we see light") and the Nicene Creed ("light from light") to affirm that the light of the Father and the Son is *one* light. And it is in the Spirit, Gregory suggests, that we comprehend this light. The source of the divine radiance that we encounter is the Father, and from the Father's light we perceive the Son's light.

We see a similar instinct at work in another fourth-century text, Athanasius's *Letters to Serapion*. In that text, Athanasius points to the Son, the radiance of the Father, as the one who enlightens the Spirit within us—like Gregory, aiming to establish the full divinity of the Spirit. Athanasius writes: "Thus the Father is Light and his Radiance is the Son . . . and so we are also permitted to see in the Son the Spirit in whom we are enlightened. . . . But when we are enlightened in the Spirit, it is Christ who enlightens us in him."[5] Athanasius thus envisions a mutual activity between the Son

---

4. Gregory of Nazianzus, *Oration 31 (Fifth Theological Oration)*, 3 (p. 118 in the Wickham translation). Original emphasis.

5. Athanasius, *Letters to Serapion*, 1.19.3–4 (p. 82 in the DelCogliano, Radde-Gallwitz, and Ayres translation).

and the Spirit that enables us to perceive the divine light. It is "in" the Spirit that we see the Son as the radiance of the Father, and yet our Spirit-enabled gaze upon the Son also enables us to perceive the Spirit (Athanasius draws explicitly on Ephesians 1:17–18 here). And the Spirit's enlightenment is itself an action initiated by the Son (here Athanasius points to John 1:9). It is worth observing a subtle difference between these two fourth-century texts at this stage. Gregory describes the object of our vision in the Spirit as the light of the Son, and the light of the Son is "from" the light of the Father. By contrast, Athanasius conceives the light we perceive as that of the Father which is mediated through the Son as the radiance of the Father (Heb 1:3), with that perception again enabled by the Spirit.

Athanasius's framing hints at the second conceptual move that was employed to describe how finite creatures might perceive the light of the God the Father. This second move is to work with the analogy of the sun. This image of the sun's light does two important things: first, it helps to convey some sense of how the divine persons may share in the light in distinct ways. Second, it also suggests how we might perceive the light of the Father in a manner that respects the Father's transcendence. An especially striking use of this approach appears in John of Damascus's *Exposition of the Christian Faith*. In that text, the Damascene appeals to the sun to convey the notion that the Son (the rays) and the Holy Spirit (the brightness) both have their eternal origin in the Father:

> One should know that we do not say that the Father is of anyone, but we do say that He is the Father of the Son. We do not say that the Son is a cause or a father, but we do say that He is from the Father and is the Son of the Father. And we do say that the Holy Ghost is of the Father and we call Him the Spirit of the Father. Neither do we say that the Spirit is from the Son, but we call Him the Spirit of the Son—"Now if any man have not the Spirit of Christ," says the divine Apostle, "he is none of his." We also confess that He was manifested and communicated to us through the Son, for "He breathed," it says, "and he said to his disciples: Receive ye the Holy Ghost." It is just like the rays and brightness coming from the sun, for the sun is the source of its rays and brightness and the brightness is communicated to us through the rays, and that it is which lights us and is enjoyed by us. Neither do we say that the Son is of the Spirit, nor, most certainly, from the Spirit.[6]

---

6. John of Damascus, *An Exact Exposition of the Orthodox Faith*, I.8, in *Writings*, 188.

We might note a couple of things about this passage. First, even though it is through the ray that the brightness is mediated to us, both the ray and the brightness (*ellampsis*) find their source in the sun. Similarly, the Son as the ray of the Father's light brings the Spirit to us, who makes us shine in the divine light. In this way, John concludes that the Son brings the light of the Father to us and the Spirit reflects that light both upon and within us. Second, John also draws from this picture a sort of grammar of trinitarian prepositions: we may speak of the Spirit *of* the Son (since the Spirit is imparted to us through the Son), but should not speak of the Spirit *from* the Son (since the Father is the eternal source of both the Son and the Spirit) or the Son *of* the Spirit (again since the Spirit is imparted to us through the Son and not the other way around).

Another text from Athanasius shows a similar dynamic at work. In *De Decretis*, he takes the light and the radiance (*apaugasma*) of the sun as a fitting cue to insist on the unity between the Father and the Son. He writes, "Here again, the illustration of light and its radiance is in point. Who will presume to say that the radiance is unlike and foreign to the sun? Rather who, thus considering the radiance relatively to the sun, and the identity of the light, would not say with confidence, 'Truly the light and the radiance are one, and the one is manifested in the other, and the radiance is in the sun, so that whoso sees this, sees that also?'"[7] The use of the image of the sun, therefore, enables Athanasius to convey the unity between the Father and the Son in a manner that could be clearly understood. In fact, it was in reflecting on this passage that G. L. Prestige could suggest that "the metaphor of radiance and light was the traditional expression of divine unity."[8] Still, while insisting that radiance is one with the sun, Athanasius is able to maintain the distinction between them. Just as anyone can see the unity of the sun and its radiance, so also is it clear that the radiance manifests the sun to us and that the sun is the source of the radiance. To reverse that order of generation would be inconceivable.

The light to which we are drawn, then, is *the light of God the Father manifested to us in the Son and perceived in the Holy Spirit*. Therefore, just as the source of light is identified with the rays jointly as one light, so also people were truly seeing God when they saw Jesus. And yet we should also recognize a paradox that we experience in an encounter with bright light. The light illuminates our surroundings and draws our attention. But to look

---

7. Athanasius, *De Decretis*, V.24, in *Select Works and Letters*, 166.
8. Prestige, *God in Patristic Thought*, 214.

directly at the source is to risk blinding oneself. We teach our children not to look directly into the sun or a flashlight, yet we teach this to them precisely as we are introducing them to the joy of light. This light, which captures our attention and enables us to see our surroundings, is also a sobering reality that requires caution and respect. Just as there is a sense of mystery and inaccessibility to the source of a light such as the sun, so also the direct perception of the Father is not available to finite and fallen creatures. It is by grace, then, that the Son mediates this light to us and the Spirit enables us to draw near its brilliance. The combination of awe and allure in the divine light is beautifully captured in Habakkuk 3:3–4: "His splendor covers the heavens, And the earth is full of His praise. His radiance is like the sunlight; He has rays flashing from His hand, And the hiding of His might is there."[9] The sun is both brilliant and imposing, and there is likewise a note of reverence that comes across unmistakably in this passage describing the divine light. As much as we need and are drawn to the light, an encounter with it will inevitably transform us.

Movement: Toward the Luminous Darkness

When we are drawn to the allure of the divine light, we are thereby changed. God both calls forth and enables our movement toward the source of that light. Recognizing this helps us to get one thing very clear at the outset of the second progression of this chapter: when we speak of movement, we are speaking of the movement of *creatures*. And while all creation is subject to transformation in the light of God, we will focus here on human beings in particular as creatures made in the image of God. In the particular sense in which we are using the term movement, then, we ascribe that term to ourselves and not to God. The present chapter will address the dynamics of movement in the divine-human encounter, particularly as it relates to the doctrine of an immutable and transcendent God. Chapter 4 will devote more explicit attention to the specific experience of that transformation on the part of human beings as we explore the way of salvation.

The suggestion that it is *we* who move (and not God) naturally invites all sorts of potential for misunderstanding, so it is worth clarifying just what we mean by movement in this chapter. The first clarification is that movement here does not mean agency. God acts in the world in all sorts

---

9. NASB translation. The NRSV, which is typically used in this book, renders the phrase at the beginning of verse 4: "The brightness was like the sun".

of ways; the very economy of salvation depends on this affirmation. Thus it is perfectly appropriate to speak of God moving in a given community or circumstance; say, in a powerful experience of worship. I certainly do not wish to deny this important use of the language of movement; I simply wish to point out that it is a different use of that language than the one I am employing here. The second clarification is that I am not advocating a static picture of the divine nature that would undermine the witness of the tradition regarding the intra-trinitarian relations. The eternal generation of the Son and the procession of the Spirit are central aspects of the Christian doctrine of God. It would be a mistake, therefore, to suppose that this trinitarian vision is incompatible with the affirmation that God does not move in the particular sense we are considering.

I am using the term movement in this chapter, by contrast, in the Aristotelian sense of change. Something that is moved in this sense makes some transition from potentiality to actuality. But God is not moved in *this* sense, as God is eternally perfect—pure act, in the words of Thomas Aquinas, without any potentiality. This means that God is immutable and that change is a mark of God's creation rather than of the Creator. Thomas puts it this way: "Everything which is moved acquires something by its movement, and attains to what it had not attained previously. But since God is infinite, comprehending in Himself all the plentitude of perfection of all being, He cannot acquire anything new, nor extend Himself to anything whereto He was not extended previously. Hence movement in no way belongs to Him."[10] As we reflect on the change involved in an encounter with the divine light, therefore, we are reflecting on a change *in creatures*. We experience movement in this respect as we are brought deeper into the light of the immutable God.

One more important clarification is in order. Lest we begin to think of this movement in Pelagian terms—that is, that we have the power to change ourselves—we must insist that it is enabled by divine grace. We do not walk toward the light on our own power, but rather we are drawn and empowered by the grace of God. Keeping in mind our claim about God's agency above, we might say that God moves us but is not moved. That is, the distinction between "moves" as a transitive verb and as an intransitive verb is instructive here. Using the transitive verb, I might say that I move a pencil on my desk. Using the intransitive verb, I might say that I need to move, and then follow through by getting up from my desk. That

10. Aquinas, *Summa Theologiae*, I.9.1 (pp. 75–76 in the Shapcote translation).

distinction helps us get clearer on the claims we are making in this chapter. God does not move or change in the sense of an intransitive verb, but God does change us in the sense of a transitive verb. In this regard, we might say that God is the subject but not the object of the movement we have in mind.

Of course, the analogy of the pencil breaks down at an important point. Unlike my moving a pencil by changing its position, God's gracious movement upon and within us is empowering or enabling. An inanimate object such as a pencil is entirely passive in its movement; it simply ends up where I put it. By contrast, human beings have a will that is both created by and healed by the light of God's grace. Our movement in the divine light is a combination of the gracious empowerment of God that makes such movement possible and our grace-enabled response. The eighteenth-century Anglican John Wesley reflected a great deal on the dynamics of divine grace and human response, even appealing to the image of light in this passage from his sermon "The Scripture Way of Salvation":

> The salvation which is here spoken of might be extended to the entire work of God, from the first dawning of grace in the soul till it is consummated in glory. If we take this in its utmost extent it will include all that is wrought in the soul by what is frequently termed "natural conscience," but more properly, "preventing grace";—all the "drawings" of the Father, the desires after God, which, if we yield to them, increase more and more; all that "light" wherewith the Son of God "enlighteneth every one that cometh into the world," *showing* every man "to do justly, to love mercy, and to walk humbly with his God"; all the *convictions* which His Spirit, from time to time, works in every child of man.[11]

The dynamics of movement in the light are here outlined in trinitarian terms: God the Father draws us by the light of the Son, who shows us what it means to walk with God, and by the prompting and power of the Spirit, who works within us to bring us deeper into that light. Wesley's sermon further makes it clear that, even though we could not respond without this work of divine grace, a response of the grace-enabled will is indeed necessary to proceed toward consummation in glory.

Once undertaken, that journey is not without its surprises. One of the striking features of the witness of the Christian tradition to the movement into the divine light is the imagery of darkness along the way. While

11. John Wesley, "The Scripture Way of Salvation," I.1–2, in Collins and Vickers, *The Sermons of John Wesley*, 583, original emphasis.

we might expect an ever-increasing experience of brightness, this is not always the case. Particularly surprising is the observation that imagery of both light and darkness shows up with reference to God. This even surfaces in biblical texts. For example, alongside the Isaiah 60 and Habakkuk 3 texts on the divine radiance we explored above, we might note the beginning of Psalm 27: "The LORD is my light and my salvation—whom shall I fear?" Yet we see a rather different picture when the people of Israel surrounded Mt. Sinai in Exodus 20:21: "The people stood at a distance, while Moses drew near to the thick darkness where God was." In this account, the presence of God is represented by darkness and fear, in contrast to Psalm 27, where the same God is conceived as the light that casts out fear. Moses's address to the Israelites in Deuteronomy 5 recounts the encounter on the mountain, noting that the Lord spoke "from the midst of the fire, the cloud, and the thick darkness" (v. 22). We find a particularly interesting example at the beginning of Psalm 97, where both of these images are combined in the portrait of a thunderstorm. This text brings the darkness of clouds and the brightness of lightning together to convey the power of God:

> The LORD is king! Let the earth rejoice;
> let the many coastlands be glad!
> Clouds and thick darkness are all around him;
> righteousness and justice are the foundation of his throne.
> Fire goes before him,
> and consumes his adversaries on every side.
> His lightnings light up the world;
> the earth sees and trembles.

We can safely conclude that, biblically speaking, an encounter with God can involve both an experience of light and an experience of darkness.

What can we make of this apparently conflicting imagery? We might begin by acknowledging that each of these images has been picked up by different voices in the tradition. Kallistos Ware notes that some figures gravitate toward one or the other: "According to their preference for the one 'sign' or the other, mystical writers may be characterized as either 'nocturnal' or 'solar.'"[12] He also suggests that some writers combine the images

---

12. Ware, *The Orthodox Way*, 126. Ware identifies Clement of Alexandria, Gregory of Nyssa, and St. Dionysius the Areopagite as those who prefer the sign of darkness and Origen, Gregory of Nazianzus, Evagrius, Pseudo-Macarius, Symeon the New Theologian, and Gregory Palamas as those who primarily use the sign of light.

of light and darkness,[13] reflecting the sort of dynamic that we saw above with Psalm 97. Recognizing this, of course, only intensifies our question: how can it be that an encounter with a God who is light would be marked by darkness? We can only make progress in answering this question by paying attention to those texts that have made use of the sign of darkness. By attending to the particular ways in which the darkness imagery functions, we can get our bearings for a theology of divine radiance that does not ignore an important stream of biblical and theological witness.

The first thing that we should notice about the biblical texts above that refer to darkness is that the darkness *surrounds* God. The darkness is not identified with God directly. Those texts refer to darkness being *around* God or God speaking *out of* darkness. The Exodus 20 passage reveals darkness as the condition of the place where God was encountered by Moses, but it does not imply that darkness should be ascribed directly to God's nature. Ware reads this text as affirming God's presence *in* darkness: "It is significant that in this passage it is not stated that God *is* darkness, but that he *dwells* in darkness."[14] This observation does not completely remove the tension between these biblical texts and those texts that emphasize God as light. Indeed, we feel that tension when we compare Exodus 20:21 to a text such as 1 John 1:5: "God is light and in him there is no darkness at all." But there is also a sense in which the juxtaposition of these texts illuminates each of them. Again, the positioning of prepositions becomes decisive. With Exodus, we can affirm that God can be present in (at least a kind of) darkness, and with 1 John, we can affirm that darkness is not present in God.

The parenthetical allusion to different kinds of darkness leads naturally to a second observation. We might be a bit more precise to say that the image of darkness gets used in different ways in Scripture. Thus, darkness functions in one way in Exodus and in another way in the Johannine literature of the New Testament. Johannine texts tend to take darkness as an indication of sin or the absence of God (such as in John 3:19 or 1 John 2:9–11). We might note a variation of this in Pauline appeals to darkness that generally emphasize the cognitive dimension of sin, combining a distortion of the mind with rebellion against God (e.g., Rom 1:21; Eph 4:18). In these examples, it is clear that darkness is something to be avoided in the journey into the life of God. But something different is clearly going on in

13. Ware, *The Orthodox Way*, 128.
14. Ware, *The Orthodox Way*, 126, original emphasis.

the passages in Exodus and Deuteronomy. Those texts envision darkness as part of the condition of the encounter with God. In this regard, darkness is not meant to convey a rebellion against God but rather a reality that attends the encounter of the finite with the infinite.[15] When finite creatures come into the presence of the infinite light, their inability to apprehend the fullness of that light is experienced as a kind of darkness. In the presence of the transcendent God, it is apparent that we are not able to know or take in all that is before us. That, it seems, is the implication of the reference to darkness in the Sinai texts.

The imagery of darkness as attending an encounter with God, then, plays an apophatic role. It reminds us that the deeper we go in the life of faith, the more we are aware of how little we know. This theme is picked up rather dramatically by Gregory Nyssa in his *Life of Moses*. In that work, Gregory describes the journey to union with God as moving in a surprising direction: from light to darkness. He suggests that "religious knowledge comes at first to those who receive it as light. Therefore what is perceived to be contrary to religion is darkness, and the escape from darkness comes about when one participates in light."[16] As one progresses, however, one comes to an increasing sense of the incomprehensibility of the divine. "This is the true knowledge of what is sought"; he continues, "this is the seeing that consists in not seeing, because that which is sought transcends all knowledge, being separated on all sides by incomprehensibility as by a kind of darkness."[17] Gregory concludes that the account of Moses seeing God in the darkness indicated that he had come to sense that "what is divine is beyond all knowledge and comprehension."[18] The imagery of darkness for Gregory means that movement toward union with God brings with it a sense of the incomprehensibility of God, even as an awareness of God's presence increases. Vladimir Lossky suggests that this does not mean for Gregory a direct experience of darkness (as we find in St. John of the Cross, for example) so much as the use of a vivid image of divine transcendence: "The infinite and never completed character of this union with

15. Vladimir Lossky offers a similar distinction between biblical accounts of darkness, some pejorative and some not, in *In the Image and Likeness of God*, 32.

16. Gregory of Nyssa, *The Life of Moses* 2.162 (p. 94 in the Malherbe and Ferguson translation).

17. Gregory of Nyssa, *The Life of Moses* 2.163 (p. 94 in the Malherbe and Ferguson translation).

18. Gregory of Nyssa, *The Life of Moses*, 2.164 (p. 94 in the Malherbe and Ferguson translation).

the transcendent God is signified by darkness, which seems to be, for St. Gregory of Nyssa, a metaphor whose purpose is to remind us of a dogmatic fact."[19]

A similar use of darkness imagery appears in the work of Pseudo-Dionysius. Across his writings, we see an account of the journey toward union with God marked by an interplay of knowing and unknowing and of light and darkness. We might take his *Mystical Theology* as an instructive example. In its opening lines, we see the juxtaposition of darkness and light that is characteristic of Pseudo-Dionysius:

> Trinity!! Higher than any being,
>> Any divinity, any goodness!
> Guide of Christians
>> in the wisdom of heaven!
> Lead us up beyond unknowing and light,
>> up to the farthest, highest peak
>> Of mystic scripture,
>> where the mysteries of God's Word
>> lie simple, absolute and unchangeable
>> in the brilliant darkness of a hidden silence.
> Amid the deepest shadow
>> they pour overwhelming light
>> on what is most manifest.
> Amid the wholly unsensed and unseen
>> they completely fill our sightless minds
>> with treasures beyond all beauty.[20]

Like Gregory of Nyssa, Pseudo-Dionysius proceeds by considering Moses's ascent up the mountain into darkness. After recounting Moses's entry "into the truly mysterious darkness of unknowing,"[21] Pseudo-Dionysius exhorts readers to strive for a similar experience: "I pray we could come to this darkness so far above light! If only we lacked sight and knowledge so as to see, so as to know, unseeing and unknowing, that which lies beyond all vision and knowledge."[22] It is clear at this stage that this darkness above light is not to be taken as a description of the divine nature, but rather as an acknowledgment of God's transcendence and our corresponding incapacity to perceive God directly. This is reinforced at the end of the work, as

19. Lossky, *In the Image and Likeness of God*, 38.
20. Pseudo-Dionysius, *The Mystical Theology*, I.1 (p. 135 in the Luibheid translation).
21. Pseudo-Dionysius, *The Mystical Theology*, I.3 (p. 137 in the Luibheid translation).
22. Pseudo-Dionysius, *The Mystical Theology*, II.1 (p. 138 in the Luibheid translation).

Pseudo-Dionysius claims in the midst of a strongly apophatic passage that the cause of all is neither darkness nor light.[23] Rather than ascribing these images to God in any direct sense, he points rather to the failure of any image to capture the transcendent reality of the divine. Lossky detects in the work of Pseudo-Dionysius as a whole a correspondence between the darkness-light pairing and the distinction between God's unknowable essence and God's energies. This distinction would play a prominent role in the work of Gregory Palamas—though, as Lossky notes, without the imagery of darkness playing such an important role.[24]

What conclusions might we draw from this exploration of darkness, particularly in relation to our overall interest in movement into the light? First, imagery of darkness that attends an encounter with God is *noetic rather than ontological*. Darkness is not to be ascribed to God's being in any respect. Rather, the references to darkness in the biblical and theological tradition serve to emphasize that God is not to be directly identified with the sensible world. As we are drawn toward the light of God, the change we experience makes us ever more acutely aware of the divine transcendence. "The uncreated Light of God," Iain MacKenzie contends, "both reveals and conceals."[25] Second, our movement toward is God characterized by paradoxes, as the interplay of light and darkness suggests. We saw this in Pseudo-Dionysius in particular, whose phrase "brilliant darkness" at the beginning of *The Mystical Theology* captures this tension. Gregory of Nyssa used a similar phrase in *The Life of Moses* in pondering the inspiration for the claim in John 1:18 that "no one has ever seen God." Gregory suggests that John the Sublime asserted this after penetrating "into the luminous darkness."[26] The brilliant darkness, the luminous darkness; such phrases suggest that even the disorientation of encountering the transcendent God is an experience of bliss. We thus turn to our third progression.

Joy: Beholding the Beauty of the Lord

One observation in our last section prompts a question: why might Pseudo-Dionysius see Moses's ascent into darkness as something to be emulated?

23. Pseudo-Dionysius, *The Mystical Theology*, V.1 (p. 141 in the Luibheid translation).

24. Lossky, *In the Image and Likeness of God*, 41–43.

25. MacKenzie, *The "Obscurism" of Light*, 109.

26. Gregory of Nyssa, *The Life of Moses*, 2.163 (p. 94 of the Malherbe and Ferguson translation).

Typically, a journey into darkness is seen as something to be avoided, so why should one pray for such an experience? It can only be concluded that the journey up the mountain leads to joy. Our reflections above indicated that the references to the darkness of Sinai are pointers to divine transcendence. Thus the movement into that darkness suggests that one is moving closer to the God who transcends sensible things. Since God is infinite in all perfections, including infinite goodness, we should not be surprised to find that this is a movement into bliss. Even for figures like Gregory of Nyssa or Pseudo-Dionysius, the awareness of divine transcendence is fully compatible with the joy of union with God. In fact, Lossky detects in Gregory the conviction that our experience of unknowing deepens our desire for union with God: "It is precisely consciousness of the radical lack of correspondence between the creature and God which makes union preferable to knowledge."[27] While the movement toward union depends initially on the knowledge made possible by divine revelation, that movement gives way gradually to an increasing sense that the essence of God is unknowable. Yet that awareness corresponds to a deepening union of love with God that is experienced as pure bliss.

We find a particularly moving account of this increasing joy in *The Life of Moses*. In reflecting on Moses's lofty experiences that left him shining in glory, Gregory notes that Moses still desired more. Even though Moses was filled to capacity, he thirsted for more—not because of his own capacity but rather according to the being of God. Gregory continues: "Such an experience seems to me to belong to the soul which loves what is beautiful. Hope always draws the soul from the beauty which is seen to what is beyond, always kindles the desire for the hidden through what is constantly perceived. Therefore, the ardent lover of beauty, although receiving what is always visible as an image of what he desires, yet longs to be filled with the very stamp of the archetype."[28] The perception of beauty in and through what is seen draws our desire upward to the infinite and unseen source of all things, which is beauty itself. Our initial contact with the divine light reveals both knowledge and goodness. As we proceed, the light of knowledge gives way to recognition of God's ineffability, but our perception of the light

---

27. Lossky, *In the Image and Likeness of God*, 38. He sees a similar dynamic at work in Pseudo-Dionysius (p. 40).

28. Gregory of Nyssa, *The Life of Moses*, 2.231 (p. 113 in the Malherbe and Ferguson translation).

of goodness intensifies. The fulfillment of our desire for God only increases the force of that desire, drawing us deeper into the divine light.

We might conclude by returning to a text that we considered above, Psalm 27. The opening line of that psalm encapsulates the theme of this book: "The LORD is my light and my salvation." But what use is made of the image of light here? Two primary ideas emerge in the course of the psalm. One theme, probably the dominant one, is that of strength and protection against adversaries. In this regard, light is conceived as hope in the face of imminent and potentially terrifying battle. But the second theme, particularly striking given the setting of the psalm, is that of beauty. Even on the verge of war, the psalmist longs for the light of God's beauty.

> One thing I asked of the LORD,
>> that will I seek after:
> to live in the house of the LORD
>> all the days of my life,
> to behold the beauty of the LORD,
>> and to inquire in his temple.
> (Ps 27:4)

Later, in verse 8, the psalmist relays the cry of his heart to seek the face of the Lord. Even though most of the psalm is given to trust in God's protection, the highest desire expressed by the psalmist is to delight in God's beauty. The salvation found in the Lord is oriented toward a particular end: to behold the beauty of the divine light.[29] And the circle is thereby completed: the Father's light radiates in the Son upon creation, which is illuminated by the Holy Spirit. As creation is drawn toward the source of that light, those creatures made in the image of God are enabled by grace to ascend the mountain in a journey that is both brilliant and blinding. Yet they keep ascending, as their deepest desire only increases as it is fulfilled. Each step into that blinding brilliance is a step further into joy.

---

29. This claim suggests that it is possible to share the apophatic instincts of Gregory of Nyssa or Pseudo-Dionysius without rejecting the hope of the beatific vision in the life to come. The use of the image of darkness to convey divine transcendence is fully compatible with the possibility of grace to lift us to the eschatological vision of 1 John 3:2: "when he is revealed, we will be like him, for *we will see him as he is.*"

2

Creation

"The Earth Shone with His Glory"

IN A BOOK EXPLORING the image of light in Christian theology, the opening lines of the Bible should not escape our notice. The narration of the creation of the heavens and the earth in Genesis 1 begins with the observation that the earth was "a formless void" and that "darkness covered the face of the deep." Depending on how one reads verse 1, the act of bringing the world into being is either implied or narrated.[1] Either way, God's first creative act in shaping the world was to speak into the face of this dark void: "Let there be light" (v. 3). When the light immediately appeared, God "saw that the light was good" and separated it from the darkness. This distinction between the day and the night (v. 4–5) constitutes the first day, initiating a pattern of divine creative activity that recurs throughout the six days of Genesis 1. It is no doubt significant for our purposes that light comes first in this creative pattern. At a purely literary level, it is true that light's priority—that is, the distinction between day and night—is rather necessary for the narration of creation in terms of successive days. But it is certainly reasonable to draw theological significance from this as well. The first mark of God's creative power that is revealed to us as readers is the emergence of light into the darkness.

---

1. For a helpful discussion of this debate, see Hamilton, *The Book of Genesis*, 103–7. If we follow the NRSV translation ("In the beginning when God created the heavens and the earth"), then the creation of light is the first divine creative act that is narrated in Scripture.

What we find in the fourth day of creation only intensifies the import of that primal light. On the fourth day, narrated in verses 14–19, we see the creation of particular lights in the sky; namely, the sun, moon, and stars. Whatever might be going on cosmologically in the distinction between the sun and a more primal light that separates the day from the night, there is something at stake in this point theologically as well. The lights of the fourth day hold practical value in providing a measure of order to guide creation, as in verse 15: "let them be for signs and for seasons and for days and years, and let them be lights in the dome of the sky to give light upon the earth." But the light of the first day is simply regarded as good, quite apart from any practical utility. The order that emerges throughout Genesis 1 is regarded as good at each step, culminating in the affirmation of verse 31 that the complete creation was "very good." But at the beginning of this pattern of creative ordering is God's calling forth of pure light declared by God to be good. By contrast with the lights of the fourth day, whose goodness appears connected to usefulness, the light of the first day is simply recognized as inherently good.

These reflections lead us to two conclusions that will help to frame this chapter on the doctrine of creation. The first is that there is a clear distinction between God and creation. It is precisely the willful creative activity of God, which is in fact verbal activity, that brings orderly shape to the formless void. The text's emphasis on God's intentional shaping of creation into something very good leaves no room for confusing the Creator and creation. The second conclusion presses in the other direction: despite this distinction, creation still reflects something of its Creator. Specifically, the goodness of creation is a direct product of the goodness of God. In this respect, we are right to note the primal light that is regarded as good and that begins the ordering of creation toward its culmination as very good. It would be too much to say that Genesis 1 envisions God as light—as we see throughout this book, there are plenty of other texts to mine for that image. Genesis 1 is in fact quite reticent to say much of anything explicitly about the nature or attributes of God. But the text is abundantly clear on the effect of God's activity: a dark and chaotic earth is transformed into a world marked by light and order.[2] And thus the goodness of creation is a direct

2. It is worth noting here that the primary roots of the doctrine of *creatio ex nihilo* in the Christian tradition are not obviously in the Genesis 1 narrative. That said, Nathan J. Chambers has recently argued that the doctrine emerged from the church's reading of Genesis 1 within the context of the two-testament Bible (see Chambers, *Reconsidering Creation Ex Nihilo*). At any rate, the debate over this question does not negate the

result of God's creative activity. The upshot is unmistakable: this light and goodness is rooted in the goodness of God.

In our exploration of the allure of the divine light reflected through creation, we will be guided by the two considerations above. The beauty of the light of creation can serve as a pointer to the divine light precisely because something of God's nature is seen in God's creation. And yet the danger of idolatry always lurks in the apprehension of the world's beauty, thereby highlighting the importance of the distinction between the creation and Creator. Our second progression, taking up the theme of movement, will examine the ways that imagery of light and darkness can shape an account of sin and disorder in creation. We will then turn to joy, our third progression, by considering the proper reception of the gifts of creation. Only in the centering of the divine light can the light reflected from the creation provide the joy befitting the good gifts of God.

Allure: Such as Might Be Perceived by Mortal Eyes

Biblical attention to manifestations of the divine radiance tends toward the particular. The light or glory of God is visible to creatures in specific places at specific times. The temple and the city of Jerusalem are especially important loci in the Old Testament, and God's radiance is most centrally manifest in the incarnation of the Son in Jesus in the New Testament. Yet we also find indications in Scripture that the divine glory shines through creation itself. "The heavens are telling the glory of God," proclaims Psalm 19:1, "and the firmament proclaims his handiwork." Psalm 97 suggests that we see not only the divine glory but also God's righteousness in creation. Verse 6 reads: "The heavens proclaim his righteousness; and all the peoples behold his glory." The theme of divine attributes being attested by creation is picked up with particular detail in Romans 1:20: "Ever since the creation of the world his eternal power and divine nature, invisible though they are, have been understood and seen through the things he has made." An especially striking example appears in Ezekiel 43, as a particular manifestation of the divine glory illuminates the surrounding earth. The vision of the glory of God coming from the east to fill the temple prompts a remarkable observation in verse 2: "the sound was like the sound of mighty waters; and the earth shone with his glory." Here creation shines because of the

importance of that doctrine for the Christian faith. There remain strong biblical and theological grounds for affirming that God created the world out of nothing.

luminous glory of God returning to the temple. Thus the movement of attention can flow in both directions. Beholding creation can lead us to an apprehension of God's glory, power, and eternal nature, and an encounter with the divine presence can illuminate creation with the sheer magnificence of God's radiance.

Light becomes a particularly valuable image of the beauty of creation in patristic commentaries on a text that we explored above, Genesis 1. In his second homily on the Hexaemeron, St. Basil centers on beauty as the main category for making sense of light as the first creation of God: "The first word of God created the nature of light, did away with the darkness, put an end to the gloom, brightened up the world, and bestowed upon all things in general a beautiful and pleasant appearance. The heavens, so long buried in darkness, appeared, and their beauty was such as even yet our eyes bear witness to."[3] He goes on to suggest that light enables a creaturely joy that cannot be surpassed by anything imaginable: "'Let there be light.' In truth, the command was itself the act, and a condition of nature was produced than which it is not possible for human reasonings to conceive anything more delightfully enjoyable."[4] Basil does not explicitly make the connection between this created light and light as an image of God. But it is scarcely a stretch to see such a connection implied, particularly given the exalted language of delight that he uses. Human minds cannot conceive of a delight greater than the illuminated creation, but there is in fact a greater joy that is beyond comprehension; namely, the joy of beholding the divine light. The illumination of creation in beauty—that our eyes can even yet behold, Basil suggests—is the work of a God who is infinite light and the source of all joy.

The connection between the first created light and the divine light that is implied in Basil is made explicitly by St. Ambrose. In his second homily on the six days of creation, Ambrose suggests that it is only natural for God to begin the ordering of creation with light, given the divine nature.

> He said: "Be light made." Whence should the voice of God in Scripture begin, if not with light? Whence should the adornment of the world take its beginning, if not from light? There would be no purpose in the world if it were not seen. In fact, God Himself

---

3. Basil, *Homily 2 on the Hexaemeron*, 6 (p. 31 in the Way translation). For more on Basil's reflections on beauty in this homily, see MacKenzie, *The "Obscurism" of Light*, 17–18.

4. Basil, *Homily 2 on the Hexaemeron*, 7 (p. 32 in the Way translation).

was in the light, because He "dwells in light inaccessible," and He "was the true light that enlightens every man who comes into this world." But He wishes the light to be such as might be perceived by mortal eyes.[5]

The God who dwells in inaccessible light (here Ambrose refers to 1 Timothy 6:16) and who is the true light (John 1:9) desired that light to be perceived by creatures. Therefore, the primal light that infuses creation makes it possible for mortals to perceive something of the Creator. And like Basil, Ambrose focuses on beauty as the proper mode for making sense of this light: "God, therefore, is the Author of light and the place and cause of darkness is the world. But the good Author uttered the word 'light' so that He might reveal the world by infusing brightness therein and thus make its aspect beautiful."[6] From the very beginning, the beauty of creation as illuminated by created light served a purpose: that creatures might perceive the goodness and beauty of the Creator in the world around them. The luminous heavens and earth, however attractive, were never meant to be the ultimate object of our adoration.

Jaroslav Pelikan sees a consistent biblical and theological theme in this connection between the divine light and the light of creation. He writes:

> Thus in the imagery of the Bible "light" is both a term for God and the name of the first among the creatures of God. *Fiat lux* provided Christian theology from the very outset with an image for speaking at the same time about the nature of God himself and about the meaning of his creative act. The language of the Bible spoke about God as light and the world as light, not merely about God as light and the world as darkness. Consideration of this usage seemed almost to compel Christian theologians to look for analogies between Creator and creature, and not merely to emphasize the discontinuity between the holy Creator and the fallen creature.[7]

Pelikan's use of the word "merely" is significant, as he thereby points to the tension between continuity and discontinuity in God's relationship to creation. This tension, which runs through the entire Christian doctrine

5. Ambrose, *Six Days of Creation*, Book 1, chapter 9, 33 (p. 38 in the Savage translation).

6. Ambrose, *Six Days of Creation*, Book 1, chapter 9, 33 (p. 39 in the Savage translation).

7. Pelikan, *Light of the World*, 39–40.

of creation, suggests that two errors must be avoided. On the one hand, the crucial distinction between God and creation should not be taken as a reason to deny the essential goodness of what God created. It would be an odd turn of events indeed if God's creatures were to reject God's own assessment that the completed creation was "very good." And as Ambrose indicates above, in a claim echoed by Pelikan, the goodness of creation is ultimately a pointer to the goodness of God.

On the other hand, it is precisely this reflection of the Creator in the created world that poses a different danger; namely, that of idolatry. Given its allure, the light of creation always threatens to draw the attention of creatures as an *end* rather than as a *pointer* to the divine light. While the goodness of creation is to be welcomed and enjoyed as the gift of God, the concentration of attention and affection that marks human worship should never be focused on this gift. Rather, the illumined creation shines with the glory of the one who made it, and its light aims to draw our focus to the Creator alone as our end. This is fitting for creatures because only the uncreated God is worthy of worship. That alone is sufficient reason for a Christian to avoid idolatry at all costs. Yet, as St. Augustine notes, there is also a certain practical wisdom in refusing to treat creation as our final end. Because its beauty pales in comparison to eternal being, the created world simply cannot satisfy our deepest longings. In his *Confessions*, Augustine reflects on this topic in a conversation with his mother just before her death: "The conversation led us towards the conclusion that the pleasure of the bodily senses, however delightful in the radiant light of this physical world, is seen by comparison with the life of eternity to be not even worth considering. Our minds were lifted up by an ardent affection towards eternal being itself."[8] For Augustine, it is perfectly reasonable to affirm the beauty of the created world while acknowledging that it is not our end.

Here we find the image of light to be, yet again, especially helpful. The beauty of creation is only evident insofar as it reflects light. This is true both of the physical, created light of which Basil spoke and of the glory of the uncreated God envisioned in Ezekiel 43. In both cases, the world's beauty is not self-generated. Rather, that beauty directs the attention of creatures to the God who both gave the world its orderly form and illuminated it so that it might be perceived. In the presence of this light, we can receive creation joyfully even as we focus our adoration on the one who made it—we will explore that posture further in the section on joy below. But first, we must

8. Augustine, *Confessions*, IX.x.24 (p. 171 in the Chadwick translation).

acknowledge a question that has been lurking throughout this discussion: how can we make sense of the persistent darkness that looms in creation? For the biblical witness makes clear that God's creatures did not continue to bask in light unabated. The danger of idolatry became a reality, casting an unmistakable shadow over the goodness and beauty of creation. While the divine light can never be extinguished, the ability of creatures to perceive it was compromised by sin. Further, the human experience of creation was deeply complicated, such that the order envisioned by the Genesis 1 account gave way to compounding disorder. In the presence of darkness, even the beauteous creation could bring suffering. In order to rediscover and fulfill their created purpose, human beings needed something to change in the very fiber of the universe. And such a movement could only be enabled by divine grace.

Movement: Out of Darkness into His Marvelous Light

In chapter 1, we explored the biblical theme of darkness that appears in references to Israel's Sinai experience. In those texts, an experience of darkness attends an encounter with God, often conveyed in the image of darkness surrounding God. We noted that this biblical stream was an important source of reflection for theologians such as Gregory of Nyssa and Pseudo-Dionysius, who took the darkness around God as an apophatic cue that God is not to be identified with the sensible world. In that respect, the biblical allusions to darkness at Sinai expressed the sense of unknowing that attends the movement of finite creatures toward union with an infinite and ineffable God. In the present chapter, we turn to a very different use of darkness imagery in Scripture. For there is another important stream of biblical material that envisions sin in its various forms as darkness. Exploring these texts will enable us to consider the brokenness of creation in relation to our guiding theme of light as well as the movement that is needed in order to return from darkness to light.

We might consider four basic categories of biblical texts that conceive sin in terms of darkness. In each case, we see a corruption of the very good order of the completed creation that was inaugurated with the calling forth of a primal light. A first category uses the image of darkness to convey a way of life that is marked by evil deeds and a rebellion against God's good order. These passages emphasize the willful dimension of sin as opposition to God's purposes. A second category includes texts that portray the condition or experience of a broken world as darkness. The emphasis here is on the effects of sin, particularly in its spiritual and cognitive dimensions. Third, we might identify passages that use darkness to allude to external evil, often in emphasizing God's capacity and promise to overcome these forces of darkness that have long troubled God's people. Finally, a fourth category involves texts that speak of divine judgment in terms of darkness. Here the willful refusal to receive the divine light amounts to an inability to share in eternal being, such that darkness becomes an image of the resulting loss of participation in life that is truly life.

We might begin our exploration of the first category, darkness as a way of life, with 1 Peter 2:9. In one respect, this is perhaps the most general of texts that use the image of darkness to refer to the pattern of life that God's people leave behind. This is simply because it does not specify particular acts so much as it emphasizes the sheer generosity of divine grace in forming a people set apart. In contrast to those who "do not believe" (v. 7) and "stumble because they disobey the word" (v. 8), verse 9 addresses God's own people: "But you are a chosen race, a royal priesthood, a holy nation, God's own people, in order that you may proclaim the mighty acts of him who called you out of darkness into his marvelous light." Still, this passage is both preceded by and followed by brief catalogues of particular behaviors and patterns that exemplify this contrast. At the beginning of 1 Peter 2, readers are exhorted to rid themselves of malice, guile, insincerity, envy, and slander. The chapter goes on to specify marks of the life proper to people who have been brought into God's marvelous light, including the resistance of destructive desires of the flesh (v. 11) and honorable conduct among the gentiles (v. 12–17). While the emphasis of the passage is on God's merciful action in Christ, there is still an indication of both the life of darkness that has been left behind and life in the light of God.

The use of darkness to describe a way of life in opposition to God is particularly evident in Johannine material. Jesus's conversation with Nicodemus in John 3 is an important example, as Jesus describes the motivation of those who remain in darkness. When the light—Jesus refers to himself here—came into the world, "people loved darkness rather than light because their deeds were evil. For all who do evil hate the light and do not come to the light, so that their deeds may not be exposed" (vv. 19–20). Here darkness indicates both opposition to Jesus and hiddenness, whereas light indicates both right relation to Jesus and revelation of what is hidden. In this respect, Jesus identifies the reason why the darkness appeals to so many and why the opposition to him can be so intense. A similar approach appears in 1 John, where darkness can suggest a way of life that is contrary to fellowship with a God who is light. "If we say that we have fellowship with him while we are walking in darkness," 1 John 1:6 warns, "we lie and do not do what is true." The repeated attention to the confession of sin in the verses that follow makes it clear that walking in darkness here is conceived in terms of particular sins. Further specificity comes in the following chapter, where hating a fellow believer is identified multiple times as a mark of walking in darkness (1 John 2:9–11).

While other uses of darkness imagery are more typical of Pauline material, we do find an intriguing example of our first category in Ephesians 5. The key for our purposes is found in verses 8–9: "For once you were darkness, but now in the Lord you are light. Live as children of light—for the fruit of the light is found in all that is good and right and true." The verses that precede and follow this exhortation outline in remarkable detail the particular actions that distinguish the way of darkness from the way of light. These are often expressed in contrasting alternatives, such as speaking with thanksgiving rather than using "obscene, silly, and vulgar talk" (v. 4) or being filled with the Spirit rather than drunken debauchery (v. 18). In all of these examples from our first category, we see that the movement from darkness to light—even if made possible only by divine grace—involves a dramatic transformation in how one's life is actually lived.

A second category of biblical texts portrays the effects of sin in terms of darkness. These passages emphasize the experience of life in a broken world as being devoid of light. Hopelessness is a key mark of this condition, often in striking contrast to the hope that appears with the emergence of divine light. Isaiah, a particularly important book for considering the image of light, conveys hopelessness in terms of darkness for both Israel and the nations (Isa 8:22; 60:2). This theme gets picked up in Zechariah's prophecy over his son John the Baptist in Luke 1: "And you, child, will be called the prophet of the Most High; for you will go before the Lord to prepare his ways, to give knowledge of salvation to his people by the forgiveness of their sins. By the tender mercy of our God, the dawn from on high will break upon us, to give light to those who sit in darkness and in the shadow of death, to guide our feet into the way of peace" (v. 76–79). Here the divine light of the coming incarnate Son represents the promise of hope, particularly hope of a coming peace, for a people in darkness.

The cognitive effects of sin also come through in a number of biblical texts in this category. Often this takes the form of light being identified with spiritual sight or wisdom, and thus darkness reflects a condition of folly. Ecclesiastes 2:13–14 is one significant example: "Then I saw that wisdom excels folly as light excels darkness. The wise have eyes in their head, but fools walk in darkness." Jesus puts a similar image to use in Luke 11:33–36 (and its parallel, Matthew 6:22–23), suggesting that the lack of spiritual sight has effects on one's entire being: "Your eye is the lamp of your body. If your eye is healthy, your whole body is full of light; but if it is not healthy, your body is full of darkness. Therefore consider whether the light in you is not darkness." The last suggestion offers a further layer, indicating that it is possible for one to be deceived about the sharpness of one's own spiritual sight. Paul offers a similar warning in Romans 2:19, imploring those experts in the law who fancy themselves "a light to those who are in darkness" to consider their own violations of the law. Pelikan notes that this biblical theme became a central feature of Athanasius' understanding of the human condition. While the divine light was not affected by the fall and creation still objectively participated in God, Athanasius understood the subjective condition of the sinner to be that of one "who was unable to see the light even though it was still there."[9]

If our first two categories emphasize the human experience of sin, both in terms of willful rebellion and of the condition of life that follows, a third set of biblical texts envisions darkness as external evil. These passages emphasize the opposition and persecution that Jesus, the light of the world, and his followers encounter in a hostile world. Darkness in this sense implies a reigning power that threatens to overcome the community of disciples if they do not remain in the light. We see an example of this in John 12, after Jesus assures his hearers that "the ruler of this world will be driven out" (v. 31). While the outcome of the confrontation between light and darkness is not in doubt, Jesus's followers must still remain close to Jesus: "The light is with you for a little longer. Walk while you have the light, so that the darkness may not overtake you. If you walk in the darkness, you do not know where you are going. While you have the light, believe in the light, so that you may become children of light" (vv. 35–36). This theme is echoed in 1 John 2:8, with the claim that "the darkness is passing away and the true light is already shining." The succeeding verses identify hate and love for fellow believers as the marks, respectively, of darkness and light.

9. Pelikan, *Light of the World*, 42.

This indicates that the external darkness that is passing away can yet be ominously replicated in the community of faith if love is not at the center of its life. The gracious agency of God the Father is emphasized in Colossians 1:13, reminding readers that "he has rescued us from the power of darkness and transferred us into the kingdom of his beloved Son." In each of these texts, darkness is conceived in active terms, implying that willful opposition to God's purposes holds sway in the world in which believers find themselves.[10] While that darkness is passing away, its danger lingers for those who do not actively remain in the light.

The spiritual dimension of the powers of darkness that is implied in the foregoing texts—most directly in the reference to the ruler of this world in John 12:31—becomes more explicit in other passages. Ephesians 6:11-12 provides a clear example, leaving no doubt about the source of the powers of darkness: "Put on the whole armor of God, so that you may be able to stand against the wiles of the devil. For our struggle is not against enemies of blood and flesh, but against the rulers, against the authorities, against the cosmic powers of this present darkness, against the spiritual forces of evil in the heavenly places." The Paul of Acts makes a similar appeal in his speech before Agrippa. In narrating his own story of conversion and calling, he recounts the words of Jesus to him on the Damascus road. Paul recalls Jesus sending him to the gentiles "to open their eyes so that they may turn from darkness to light and from the power of Satan to God, so that they may receive forgiveness of sins and a place among those who are sanctified by faith in me" (Acts 26:18). There are two clear parallels here between Paul's own physical experience and the spiritual experience of the gentiles to which Jesus has sent him. First, Paul's sight had been restored just before his baptism (narrated in Acts 9:17-18), and now he recalls Jesus sending him to open the eyes of the gentiles. Second, Paul had experienced Jesus's presence as a bright light on the road to Damascus (narrated in Acts 9:3 and recounted in 26:13). Now before Agrippa, Paul describes the mission Jesus gave him in terms of turning the gentiles from darkness to light. Furthermore, Paul connects the gentiles' movement from darkness to light with a turning from the power of Satan to God. Given this biblical

10. It may be tempting to read Psalm 139:12 in similar terms: "even the darkness is not dark to you; the night is as bright as the day, for darkness is as light to you." However, the context (particularly in v. 7) implies that this is an affirmation of God's omnipresence rather than an explicit reference to a victory over a willful opposition. Still, the references to such an opposition beginning in v. 19 perhaps render this an open question of interpretation.

stream, then, we can understand the historic practice of renouncing the devil at baptism. Moving from darkness to light involves leaving behind the spiritual powers opposing God in the present condition of the world and embracing the eternal power of God.

A final category of biblical texts that relate darkness to sin focuses on divine judgment. While our second category included passages that emphasize the present human experience of a broken world, this fourth category focuses on a coming judgment from God that will be experienced as darkness. Darkness thus takes on a distinctly eschatological resonance in these texts. A well-known example can be found in Hannah's prayer in 1 Samuel 2, where she lists among a series of inversions the lot of the faithful and the wicked: "He will guard the feet of his faithful ones, but the wicked shall be cut off in darkness" (v. 9). We find strong eschatological notes in the warning of the coming day of the Lord in Zephaniah 1:15 ("a day of darkness and gloom, a day of clouds and thick darkness") as well as in the vision of the bowls of God's wrath in Revelation 16:10. When Jesus commends the faith of the centurion in Matthew 8, he suggests another coming inversion: many gentiles will come to feast with the patriarchs in the kingdom of heaven, while "heirs of the kingdom will be thrown into the outer darkness, where there will be weeping and gnashing of teeth" (v. 12). Texts in this category also warn of a particular coming judgment for those who lead God's people astray, such as the false prophets of Micah 3:5–6 or the false teachers of Jude 1:10–13. Finally, we occasionally find darkness imagery used in Wisdom literature to express a sense of undeserved judgment, such as in Job 19:8 or Psalm 44:19. In these texts, darkness seems to indicate both the lack of evident divine favor and the inability to understand why.

What might we make of this last category of passages theologically? A significant key can be found in the biblical association of God with light, which we explored in chapter 1. If sharing in the divine life involves walking in light—a recurring theme in 1 John—then the refusal to abide in the light can lead to no other outcome than darkness. In this respect we can detect a certain parallel between light and being, such that participation in God as being itself is the very basis of our own being. One thinks of Teresa of Avila's *Interior Castle*, in which we find the image of the castle of the soul with many mansions. God shines as a bright light at the center of the castle.[11] But the soul that has fallen into mortal sin is unable to perceive it. "You need know only one thing about it," she writes, "that, although the Sun

---

11. Teresa of Avila, *Interior Castle*, II.

Himself, Who has given it all its splendour and beauty, is still there in the centre of the soul, it is as if He were not there for any participation which the soul has in Him, though it is as capable of enjoying Him as is the crystal of reflecting the sun."[12] Such a state does not diminish the brightness of the light at all, however. The issue is a matter of how the soul in a state of mortal sin is able to take in what is eternally there. Teresa continues: "It should be noted here that it is not the spring, or the brilliant sun which is in the centre of the soul, that loses its splendour and beauty, for they are always within it and nothing can take away their beauty. If a thick black cloth be placed over a crystal in the sunshine, however, it is clear that, although the sun may be shining upon it, its brightness will have no effect upon the crystal."[13] In this respect, the darkness one experiences is an outcome of the sin that prevents one from experiencing the light that is continually present.

Augustine thought along similar lines, insisting that the goodness of creation is rooted in the supreme goodness of the Creator. Evil and corruption of God's good creation can only be understood as a privation of the good. To share in being at all is to participate in God, "that which truly is," as the ultimate good.[14] In a similar way, to share in light at all requires walking in the light of God who is light (to put the matter in Johannine terms). To speak of divine judgment as darkness, then, is simply to acknowledge that we can only share in the good to the degree that we abide in God as the supreme good.[15] This biblical category of darkness as divine judgment can thus be understood as a privation of light—the very light in which is found the fullness of life itself. By contrast, the movement enabled by divine grace leads God's people out of the darkness in each of the dimensions that we have traced in this biblical survey. To walk in that light is to experience God's creation in a very different way: as a gift that reflects the supreme goodness of the Creator.

12. Teresa of Avila, *Interior Castle*, II (pp. 33–34 in the Peers translation).

13. Teresa of Avila, *Interior Castle*, II (p. 34–35 in the Peers translation).

14. Augustine, *Confessions*, III.vii.12 (p. 43 in the Chadwick translation). A fuller development of these themes appears in *Confessions*, VII.xi.17–VII.xiii.19, and *Enchiridion*, chapters III–IV.

15. Granted, the Wisdom literature texts cited above pose a particular challenge here, since the narrator denies consciousness of any willful rejection of God. Still, two points are especially worth acknowledging: 1) Neither Job 19 nor Psalm 44 affirms divine injustice; they only reflect the sensation that one is experiencing divine judgment unfairly; and 2) that sensation itself can be the result of the cognitive effects of a fallen human condition. The attempt to justify oneself is a common refrain in the biblical narrative, and it highlights the need for the light of divine grace.

Joy: Source of Sweet Delight

Earlier in this chapter, we noted Ambrose's suggestion that the beauty of the world is a pointer to the goodness of the God who created it. In his *Enchiridion*, Augustine picks up this theme, noting with precision the conditioned quality of the goodness of creation: "By this Trinity, supremely and equally and immutably good, were all things created. But they were not created supremely, equally, nor immutably good. Still, each single created thing is good, and taken as a whole they are very good, because together they constitute a universe of admirable beauty."[16] We can clearly detect the echo of Genesis 1 here, as Augustine recalls the pronouncement of each discrete aspect of creation as good and the totality of the ordered creation as very good. Further, the distinction between the supreme, equal, and immutable goodness of the Holy Trinity and the contingent goodness of created things provides a cue for how creation is to be received. Every created good can be enjoyed as a reflection of God's goodness, if that good is kept in its proper order with the love of God at the center of one's affection. Augustine develops this in a key passage in *City of God*, suggesting that physical beauty

> is a good created by God, but it is a temporal, carnal good, very low in the scale of goods; and if it is loved in preference to God, the eternal, internal, and sempiternal Good, that love is as wrong as the miser's love of gold, with the abandonment of justice, though the fault is in the man, not in the gold. This is true of everything created; though it is good, it can be loved in the right way or in the wrong way—in the right way, that is, when the proper order is kept, in the wrong way when that order is upset.[17]

The grace-enabled movement explored in the previous section, then, must involve a reordering of our loves. With God the Creator at the center of our desire, the creation that had been experienced in disarray can reveal its beauty.

Our guiding image of light serves us rather well at this point. For any object of beauty to be perceived by the human eye, physical light is necessary. In a room without any light, even a stunning Guido Reni painting can only be experienced as darkness. If we extend this thought experiment to the relationship between the uncreated divine light and creation, we can

16. Augustine, *Enchiridion*, chapter III (p. 239 in the Outler translation).
17. Augustine, *City of God*, XV.22 (p. 636 in the Bettenson translation).

get a sense for how a proper orientation to God is needed to reveal the full beauty of the ordered creation. (We can detect an echo of Ambrose here, even if Ambrose was referring immediately to created light enabling the physical beauty of God's creation to be perceived.) By attending to the God who is light, we can take in the goodness of what has been made in its proper mode. We might even press the analogy one step further and recognize that there is an essential connection between physical light and the beauty of an object. It is true that light *reveals* the beauty of an object, but there is also a sense in which the beauty of an object is established in the relationship of light to the form of the object. In a similar way, it is not only that God reveals the goodness of creation, but the goodness of creation derives from its relationship to the Creator. Like all analogies, of course, this one has important limits. There is no relationship within the created order that univocally reflects the relationship between God and creation. Still, as analogies go, the relationship of physical light and the beauty of objects can point our minds in a helpful direction.

What, then, is our experience of creation when properly ordered to the supreme good of the Creator? Perceived in the light of God, creation is welcomed with joy as a gift. This is possible precisely because created things are not regarded as the source of their own goodness, but rather as a reflection of the God who is the source of infinite goodness. Augustine concludes that if God alone is sought as the source of joy, then God's gifts play their proper role in experiencing that joy. In his *Confessions*, he develops this thought in relation to his own God-given talents:

> Therefore he who made me is good, and he is my good, and I exult to him, for all the good things that I was even as a boy. My sin consisted in this, that I sought pleasure, sublimity, and truth not in God but in his creatures, in myself and other created beings. So it was that I plunged into miseries, confusions, and errors. My God, I give thanks to you, my source of sweet delight, and my glory and my confidence. I thank you for your gifts. Keep them for me, for in this way you will keep me.[18]

The tendency to seek ultimate joy in created goods narrated here corresponds to the vision of idolatry that we explored above. Just as the goodness of the world can be acknowledged without making creation an object of worship, so also can created goods be received with joy without fixating on

---

18. Augustine, *Confessions*, I.xx.31 (pp. 22–23 in the Chadwick translation).

them as ultimate. In both cases, the acknowledgment of God as source and end orients a proper relationship to the world around us.

The right ordering of created goods in light of God as the supreme good was developed with characteristic clarity by St. Thomas Aquinas. His *Summa Theologiae* includes a lengthy discourse on happiness, including a consideration and rejection of various proposed sources of ultimate happiness. At the end of this list of possibilities, he concludes that no created good can constitute human happiness. Only the object of the will, the universal good, can satisfy our deepest desire. "This is to be found," Thomas argues, "not in any creature, but in God alone; because every creature has goodness by participation. Wherefore God alone can satisfy the will of man."[19] The goods of creation are thus genuine goods, insofar as they participate in the infinite goodness of God. And for Thomas, the human will inclines toward this ultimate good such that it will not and cannot be satisfied in the end by any contingent good.

And here we return to where we began. God created the light, and the light was good. The created light shone on the rest of creation, which ultimately was declared by God to be very good. But that light, made as Ambrose suggested so that it might give mortal eyes some image of the light inaccessible, was always intended to draw the attention of human beings beyond itself and beyond the creation it illumined. In a similar way, the created world was not only recognized by God to be very good, but it derived its goodness from its Creator, who is the supreme good. With that supreme good, that inaccessible light, as the end toward which we move, the beauty of creation is seen afresh. But wandering in many forms of darkness as we are, we cannot make such a movement of our own accord. As we have seen in this chapter, that movement can only be enabled by grace. And what more sublime form could grace take than God entering into creation? The world that had been filled with the primal created light from its beginning was now about to enter a new chapter, for "the true light, which enlightens everyone, was coming into the world" (John 1:9).

---

19. Aquinas, *Summa Theologiae*, I-II.2.8.

3

Jesus

"The Son Is the Radiance of God's Glory"

AMONG THE GOSPEL ACCOUNTS of the life and ministry of Jesus, the Gospel of Luke demonstrates a unique interest in its early chapters. The narration of the events leading up to and following the births of John the Baptist and Jesus includes a number of prophecies regarding the significance of these figures. These passages frame the stories that follow in light of Israel's role in the economy of salvation. One of these narratives is especially notable for our purposes. After the birth of John the Baptist, his father Zechariah is filled with the Holy Spirit and speaks a prophetic word. After celebrating God's favor in remembering the salvation promised to Israel's ancestors, Zechariah reveals that his infant son will be a prophet of the Most High. As prophet, John will prepare the way for the Lord and give knowledge of the coming salvation to God's people. To convey the significance of what was to come, Zechariah turned to the image of light:

> By the tender mercy of our God,
> the dawn from on high will break upon us,
> to give light to those who sit in darkness and in the shadow of death,
> to guide our feet into the way of peace.
> (Luke 1:78–79)

In the next chapter, after the birth of Jesus, we encounter a similar prophecy in the form of a prayer. When Jesus's parents brought him to the temple to present him to the Lord, they met the devout and righteous man Simeon. Luke tells us that the Holy Spirit rested on Simeon and had revealed to him that he would not die before seeing the Lord's Messiah. Guided by the Spirit, Simeon entered the temple and took Jesus in his arms. He then offered a prayer, giving thanks that he could now die in peace:

> for my eyes have seen your salvation,
>   which you have prepared in the presence of all peoples,
> a light for revelation to the Gentiles
>   and for glory to your people Israel.
> (Luke 2:30–32)

While Zechariah had emphasized God's faithfulness in fulfilling the promise of salvation to Israel, Simeon celebrates the glory that comes to Israel as God's salvation extends to the nations (which Luke will go on to narrate with particular clarity in Acts). And this salvation is fulfilled in Jesus, the one for whom Zechariah's son will prepare the way and the one Simeon holds in his arms. In both cases, the emergence of Jesus into the world is understood in terms of light.

The connection between Jesus and light is every bit as direct—and, as we will see, even more pervasive—in the Gospel of John. The recurring title of "light of the world" in that gospel (John 8:12; 9:5; 11:9; 12:46) cues a central image through which readers should understand and respond to the stories of Jesus's activity and teaching. And because this image is multivalent, it provides a useful lens on many dimensions of Christology. In this chapter, we will explore the person and work of Jesus in terms of the divine light. Our first progression, allure, will focus primarily on the incarnation of the divine Son. As the radiance of the Father, Jesus offers the clearest visible manifestation of God's beauty to creatures. In the second section, on movement, our attention will turn to the ways in which Jesus's salvific work makes possible our own transformation. Finally, we will take up the transfiguration of Jesus to center our exploration of the theme of joy. In this chapter, we will consider the transfiguration from the angle of Christology, drawing out the ways this event reveals the basis of human joy in Jesus's divine identity. In chapter 4, we will explore the transfiguration from the perspective of soteriology, emphasizing its role as a glimpse of the blissful fulfillment of human transformation.

Allure: The Life Was the Light of All People

John's Gospel begins, like Genesis, with a theological account of creation. And this account of creation, again like Genesis, gives a prominent place to the theme of light. We might recall from chapter 2 the suggestion made by St. Ambrose in his second homily on the six days of creation in Genesis 1. God dwells in inaccessible light, Ambrose contended, so it makes sense that God would begin to adorn the world by creating perceptible light. This enables mortal eyes to take in something of the divine glory in a manner fitting to their capacity. Ambrose's proposition, while focused on Genesis, offers an intriguing perspective that we can bring to our reading of the opening of the Gospel of John. All things came into being through the Word who was "with God" and who "was God." And "what has come into being in him was life, and the life was the light of all people. The light shines in the darkness, and the darkness did not overcome it" (John 1:1–5). At this stage, we see in this gospel two elaborations of the divine activity of creation. First, the very good creation in its totality, imaged as light, was infused with life as a gift of God. Second, this abundant life in creation participates by its nature in the Word, through whom it came into being. John does not seem to draw a hard distinction here between the life that was brought into being and the life that the Word eternally is; rather, the former only is "the light of all people" insofar as it participates in the Word. If this is correct, then the incarnation—which John 1 proceeds to narrate—is a natural extension of the divine creative activity.

This becomes even clearer as we turn to the middle portion of John's prologue, which focuses on John the Baptist. This section (vv. 6–9) offers an interesting intertextual echo of Zechariah's prophecy in Luke 1. John the Baptist was sent by God, we read both in verse 7 and in verse 8, to testify to the light. "He himself was not the light," however, as "the true light, which enlightens everyone, was coming into the world" (v. 9). Here we must pause, for the historical particularity of the reference to John the Baptist strengthens the connection between creation and incarnation that was only hinted at in the opening verses of John's Gospel. The light that was coming into the world, to which John the Baptist would testify, was clearly the Word incarnate in Jesus. While this is the same light and life referenced in verses 1–5, it was coming into the world in a new mode—one that had not even been given in creation.

The last section of the prologue draws out the revelatory nature of the incarnation: "And the Word became flesh and lived among us, and we have seen his glory, the glory as of a father's only son, full of grace and truth" (v. 14). We thus see the same creative movement that Ambrose detected in Genesis, in which the transcendent God created light in order to give mortal eyes a glimpse of the divine glory. Now in John's prologue, the divine Word—the light of the world—takes on flesh to reveal even more fully the Father's glory. While created light had always been a mere pointer to or image of the divine beauty, in the incarnation we encounter the divine Son directly. So verse 18: "No one has ever seen God. It is God the only Son, who is close to the Father's heart, who has made him known." The incarnation confirms the creative intention of God to be known in a manner fitting to the capacity of creatures. The glory imaged in the light that adorned the world of God's creation is now seen immediately in flesh.

John's prologue is not only concerned with how we might see the divine glory despite human finitude. There is also a recognition of sin and its consequences for our perception of God's light. We see this symbolized in darkness in verse 5, as the light—representing the fullness of life brought into being by the Word—"shines in the darkness, and the darkness did not overcome it." This passage coheres nicely with the connection between light and being that we explored in chapter 2. The Johannine tendency to link light and life (as we see in verse 4) prompts us to read darkness as a rejection of the fullness of life. Yet the life and being that remained in creation, continually offered by the divine Word, could not be extinguished by the nonbeing of evil and brokenness. This tension between life and the rejection of life emerges again in verses 10–11, where the pattern of human response to creation is repeated in the response to the incarnation. This time, human resistance to the Word that followed creation leads to the outright rejection by some of the incarnate Word: "He was in the world, and the world came into being through him; yet the world did not know him. He came to what was his own, and his own people did not accept him." Yet there were also some who did receive him and believe in his name, and to them "he gave power to become children of God" (v. 12).

These reflections on the opening of John's Gospel help us to understand the incarnation as pointing both back to creation and forward to redemption. God created light first as an image of the divine glory that could be perceived by mortals, drawing them to participate in the fullness of life offered by participation in the divine Word. The incarnation of the Word extends this creative impulse, now to enable human beings to see the divine glory in flesh. Those who receive and believe in the Word-made-flesh are enabled to become children of God, sharing in the light and life that overcomes the darkness. The incarnation thus makes possible the very purpose for which they were created. As Arthur Michael Ramsey suggests,

> In Christ mankind is allowed to see not only the radiance of God's glory but also the true image of man. Into that image Christ's people are now being transformed, and in virtue of this transformation into the new man they are realizing the meaning of their original status as creatures in God's image. Thus redemption is wrought not *in vacuo* but on the groundwork of creation.[1]

As the light of the world, Jesus makes it possible for human beings both to see and to share in the eternal divine glory.

We see a similar dynamic at work in the opening verses of Hebrews. That work begins with an acknowledgment of a dual superiority of the divine Son; namely, that the Son is the highest mode of divine revelation and that the Son is properly regarded as higher in status than any creature. The latter point is made by emphasizing the superiority of the Son to angels, a comparison which is developed in 1:4–14. But the former point is made by recalling briefly the history of divine revelation leading up to the incarnation: "In the past God spoke to our ancestors through the prophets at many times and in various ways, but in these last days he has spoken to us by his Son, whom he appointed heir of all things, and through whom also he made the universe. The Son is the radiance of God's glory and the exact representation of his being, sustaining all things by his powerful word."[2] The connection between creation and incarnation comes through again in striking fashion here. The Son who is now the culmination of God's revelatory speaking is the one through whom God made the universe (another echo of John's prologue) and who sustains all things by his word. The action of God in creation and incarnation is oriented toward making God's glory perceptible to creatures. To this end, it is worth noting that John's Gospel and Hebrews both use a combination of auditory and visual images, though John seems to prefer the notion of seeing while Hebrews favors the image of divine speaking.

Our reflections thus far, focused as they have been on creation and incarnation, do not yet obviously rule out an Arian reading of these biblical texts. It would be possible to conceive of the Word as the first and highest

1. Ramsey, *The Glory of God,* 151.

2. Hebrews 1:1–3, New International Version. I use the NIV in this case because of the translation of *apaugasma* as "radiance."

creature of God and as the means through which the rest of creation came into being. On such an account, the incarnate Word would still be regarded as a creature of God rather than the eternal God himself. Thus it is crucial to emphasize that the Son or the Word is the *eternal* radiance of the Father, who always was, is, and will be fully divine. The image of light, particularly as used in relation to the sun, proves helpful in making this point. In his study of patristic reflections on the doctrine of God, G. L. Prestige notes that figures such as Origen, Eusebius, and Athanasius emphasized the eternal generation of the Son by the Father by means of the image of light. "It will be noticed," Prestige observed, "that the relation between Son and Father is compared to that between light and light; a continuous process is hinted at, if not expressly stated, since the projection of ray from sun is a continuous process."[3] We recall here our discussion in chapter 1 of the role of light in the trinitarian reflections of Gregory of Nazianzus, Athanasius, and John of Damascus. For the latter two, the sun in particular was a useful picture of both the union and distinction involved in the Father's eternal begetting of the Son. Jaroslav Pelikan highlights the importance of the image of the sun for Athanasius in articulating the inseparability of the light and the radiance. While it is possible to distinguish the sun and its light in our minds, he reasoned, it is inconceivable that either should exist without the other. In the same way, one can distinguish between the Father and the Son without making the fatal error of supposing that one could be without the other.[4] The allure of the incarnate Son, therefore, hinted at by the light and life offered at creation, is the very beauty of God in flesh. As Pope St. John Paul II put it in his encyclical *Veritatis splendor*, "the light of God's face shines in all its beauty on the countenance of Jesus Christ."[5] He is the eternal ray of the Father's light, now made visible to creaturely eyes as never before.

3. Prestige, *God in Patristic Thought*, 153–54.

4. Pelikan, *Light of the World*, 69. In his third chapter, Pelikan traces the development of the use of the image of the sun, recognizing its ever-increasing complexity. Notably, the image of light from light had to be detached from the image of fire from fire, since the latter was found to be more susceptible to Arian interpretations (p. 58).

5. John Paul II, *Veritatis Splendor*, 2.

Movement: Which, through Suffering, Transforms the Darkness

The glory of God made visible in Jesus, as well as the connection between creation and incarnation, come through with particular clarity in 2 Corinthians 4:6: "For it is the God who said, 'Let light shine out of darkness,' who has shone in our hearts to give the light of the knowledge of the glory of God in the face of Jesus Christ." Those who perceive that glory in Christ, we read in the previous chapter of Paul's epistle, "are being transformed into the same image from one degree of glory to another" (2 Cor 3:18). We will consider the 2 Corinthians 3 text in greater detail in our next chapter, as we explore soteriology through the image of light. In this chapter, our task is to consider in christological terms what makes our transformation possible. That is, how does the work of Jesus, the luminous face of God's glory, make it possible for human beings to share in that glory?

While the instinct to center Jesus's death and resurrection in this regard is appropriate, we should not neglect the place of his life and ministry. This is especially clear as we consider one key aspect of the image of light; namely, light as knowledge. One of the ways in which the incarnation reveals the divine glory is in Jesus's teaching ministry, which is revelatory of the nature and purposes of God. The epistemic effects of sin have left human beings in a state of ignorance, which is often cast (as we saw in chapter 2) in terms of darkness in the New Testament. The teaching ministry of Jesus brings light to dispel this ignorance and thereby illuminates the mind and soul. Of course, even as we focus on the place of knowledge in human transformation, it is crucial to avoid isolating the cognitive dimension from the whole person. We see a beautiful reflection on the connection between one's mind and one's entire life in the *Fourth Theological Oration* of Gregory of Nazianzus. Here Gregory reflects on the Son as light: "He is called 'Light,' because he is the brilliance of souls pure in mind and life. If ignorance and sin are darkness, knowledge and inspired life must be light. He is 'Life,' because he is 'Light,' constituting and giving reality to every thinking being."[6] Precisely as the Son brings light to the mind, he brings life to one's entire being as "the brilliance of souls."

The connection between knowledge, light, and life is developed in Pope Benedict XVI's study of the parables of Jesus, part of his three-volume

---

6. Gregory of Nazianzus, *Oration 30 (Fourth Theological Oration)*, 20 (p. 110 in the Wickham translation).

Jesus of Nazareth. The parables, which Benedict suggests "constitute the heart of Jesus's preaching,"[7] involve a twofold movement. On the one hand, Jesus uses the parables to bring transcendent realities into proximity. "He has to lead us to the mystery of God—to the light that our eyes cannot bear and that we therefore try to escape. In order to make it accessible to us, he shows how the divine light shines through in the things of this world and in the realities of everyday life."[8] On the other hand, that movement to make that light accessible to us calls forth a response from the hearer:

> He conveys knowledge that makes demands upon us; it not only or even primarily adds to what we know, but it changes our lives. . . . This means, though, that the parables are ultimately an expression of God's hiddenness in this world and of the fact that knowledge of God always lays claim to the whole person—that such knowledge is one with life itself, and that it cannot exist without "repentance."[9]

The emergence of light through Jesus's parables, then, invites a total commitment on the part of those hearers who wish to respond. The teaching ministry of Jesus illuminates the mind with knowledge that offers life in its fullest sense to those who hear.

In this way, we can make sense of how the recurring theme of light gets used in the Johannine corpus. Christological references to light are typically connected to a response of movement: "walking" or "following" constitute the transition from darkness to light. John 8:12 provides a clear example: "Again Jesus spoke to them, saying, 'I am the light of the world. Whoever follows me will never walk in darkness but will have the light of life.'" From the other angle, Jesus suggests that those who do not respond stand still and remain in darkness. This is precisely the fate avoided by those who put their belief in Jesus into motion: "I have come as light into the world, so that everyone who believes in me should not remain in the darkness" (John 12:46). In the same discourse, Jesus connects faithful response to the commandment that he brings from the Father, a commandment that is itself "eternal life" (12:49-50). A similar pattern emerges in the letter of 1 John. In 1 John 2, we find an elaboration of the "new commandment that is true in him and in you, because the darkness is passing away and the true light is already shining" (v. 8). That commandment centers on love shared among believers: "Whoever says, 'I am in the light,' while hating a brother

---

7. Pope Benedict XVI, *Jesus of Nazareth*, I:183.

8. Pope Benedict XVI, *Jesus of Nazareth*, I:192.

9. Pope Benedict XVI, *Jesus of Nazareth*, I:193.

or sister, is still in the darkness. Whoever loves a brother or sister lives in the light, and in such a person there is no cause for stumbling. But whoever hates another believer is in the darkness, walks in the darkness, and does not know the way to go, because the darkness has brought on blindness" (1 John 2:9–11). Here again, one demonstrates the reception of illuminating knowledge in how one lives. The way of life that reflects walking in the light is one marked by love.

For all of the importance of the teaching ministry of Jesus, his death and resurrection undoubtedly occupy a central place in his work. The transformative work of Christ opens the way for us to take up the invitation to walk in the light. Another Johannine text, 1 John 1:7, points us in this direction: "but if we walk in the light as he himself is in the light"—contextually, verse 5 suggests that the antecedent of "he himself" is God—"we have fellowship with one another, and the blood of Jesus his Son cleanses us from all sin." The reference to the blood of Jesus in this text assumes, but does not develop, an account of the atonement. Where might we turn, then, for guidance in exploring the death and resurrection of Jesus through the lens of light? Our aim here is not to commit to one particular model of the atonement among many in the Christian tradition. Rather, we are after a way of understanding the cross and resurrection in relation to imagery of light and darkness.

It makes sense to turn first to the passion narratives in the Gospels, and particularly in the Synoptic Gospels, which are punctuated at key moments with darkness. After the Passover meal, the action moves out into the night, where Jesus prays a short distance from his disciples (Matt 26:30–46; Mark 14:26–42; Luke 22:39–46). The disciples' inability to stay awake heightens the reader's sense of the late hour. After Jesus's arrest moments later, he is taken to the house of the high priest. Outside, in the courtyard, Peter waits with the crowd. Luke and John mention that a fire was kindled in the courtyard for warmth, a detail that signals the coldness and darkness of the scene (Luke 22:55; John 18:18). Perhaps the most significant instance occurs the next day, after Jesus's trial and crucifixion. All three Synoptic Gospels note that, while Jesus is on the cross, darkness came across the land from noon until three in the afternoon (Matt 27:45; Mark 15:33; Luke 23:44–45). This period of darkness concludes with the moment of his death. We thus encounter a striking portrait: the divine light in flesh, living his final hours before death in a landscape devoid of light.

The lingering darkness throughout the passion narrative invites christological reflection. For here we see the continuing intentional movement
of the incarnate Son into the depths of the human condition. The Word
became flesh in the incarnation, reflecting the Father's glory, bringing grace
and truth into a world that did not know him (if we might draw from John
1:10–16). While some believed and received him, others rejected him with
an intensity that increases throughout the Gospel narratives. Now in his
passion Jesus willingly goes deeper, moving further into the darkness of a
world that has not received the light that brings life. While that darkness is
exemplified by those who visibly oppose him, Jesus's own disciples are not
immune to it. Peter's denials of Jesus take place in that dark courtyard outside the residence of the high priest. While Peter will be restored after the
resurrection, the denials themselves add another layer to the darkness of
the passion. Even more tragic is the betrayal of Judas, who goes out into the
night after receiving the piece of bread from Jesus (John 13:30). Benedict
notes that Judas's grief and regret over his treachery led him so deep into
darkness that he lost hope of restoration:

> His second tragedy—after the betrayal—is that he can no longer
> believe in forgiveness. His remorse turns into despair. Now he sees
> only himself and his darkness; he no longer sees the light of Jesus,
> which can illumine and overcome the darkness. He shows us the
> wrong type of remorse: the type that is unable to hope, that sees
> only its own darkness, the type that is destructive and in no way
> authentic. Genuine remorse is marked by the certainty of hope
> born of faith in the superior power of the light that was made flesh
> in Jesus.[10]

While Peter's restoration shows that light can indeed overcome the darkness, Judas's despair leaves him unwilling to turn to that redemptive light.

The movement of Jesus into the depths of human need leads to the
cross, whereupon darkness sets over the land. Here begins the pivotal
chapter in the encounter of light and darkness, one that will culminate in
the resurrection. On the cross, the light of the world enters the deepest
darkness in order to transform it through self-giving love. The darkness of
evil and injustice cannot simply be ignored by God, insists Benedict, but
rather God willingly takes reconciliation upon himself in the person of the
Son: "God himself 'drinks the cup' of every horror to the dregs and thereby
restores justice through the greatness of his love, which, through suffering,

10. Pope Benedict XVI, *Jesus of Nazareth*, II:69.

transforms the darkness."[11] The cry of dereliction becomes a particularly significant marker of this transformation. In citing the words of Psalm 22, Jesus enters into the tribulation of those who are unable to see God's light and thus brings that light into view. Again, Benedict offers insight:

> Jesus is praying the great psalm of suffering Israel, and so he is taking upon himself all the tribulation, not just of Israel, but of all those in this world who suffer from God's concealment. He brings the world's anguished cry at God's absence before the heart of God himself. He identifies himself with suffering Israel, with all who suffer under "God's darkness"; he takes their cry, their anguish, all their helplessness upon himself—and in so doing he transforms it.[12]

The only way that a condition of darkness can be transformed is through contact with light, which is precisely what is happening on the cross. But what of the moment on the cross? Is not the darkness victorious? While the resurrection will reveal the ultimate victory of the light, Benedict's reflections above show the significance of the cross itself. For those who are unable to see light and can sense only hopelessness, the cross reveals the presence of the divine Son in their midst. Not only as a promise, but as a transformative presence, the light of God enters into the anguish of a disordered creation in a movement of self-giving love. As Junius Johnson suggests, this changes our vision at our crucial moment of need. "And so we are brought to the cross," he writes, "that we may be dazzled by the brilliance that shines from there and have our eyes strengthened so that in God's light we may see light."[13]

If the cross reflects the presence of light in darkness, the resurrection of Jesus reveals the outcome of the encounter between light and darkness. Neither suffering, nor anguish, nor death itself could extinguish the light of the world. On the contrary, like a bright lamp turned on in a dark room, the flood of light chases the darkness. Here we can return to the prologue of the Gospel of John, a text in which we have already recognized themes of creation and incarnation. Now, read in light of Easter, we detect the resonance of resurrection as well: "What has come into being in him was life, and the life was the light of all people. The light shines in the darkness, and the darkness did not overcome it" (1:3–5). The connection between light

11. Pope Benedict XVI, *Jesus of Nazareth*, II:232.

12. Pope Benedict XVI, *Jesus of Nazareth*, II:214.

13. Johnson, *The Father of Lights*, 169.

and life flowing from the Word reminds us again of Jesus's divine identity. Precisely because Jesus is God, who is being itself, the nonbeing of death had no hope of prevailing over him. Darkness cannot remain in the presence of light. It is no surprise, then, that light is a pervasive feature of Easter liturgies across the ecclesial traditions. A beautiful example is found in the opening prayer of the Service of Light in the *Book of Common Prayer* of the Episcopal Church. As the first part of the Great Vigil of Easter, this service includes the lighting of a fire. The prayer reads:

> O God, through your Son you have bestowed upon your people the brightness of your light: Sanctify this new fire, and grant that in this Paschal feast we may so burn with heavenly desires, that with pure minds we may attain to the festival of everlasting light; through Jesus Christ our Lord. *Amen.*[14]

This prayer identifies the risen Jesus as the means by which God's people might come to share in the eternal divine radiance. The hope of this festival of everlasting light, which burns in the desires of those in Christ, has in the resurrection replaced the darkness of anguish and disorder.

The work of Jesus, the Word incarnate, draws human beings into the light and life that the divine Word has offered from the beginning of creation. This transformative movement out of darkness touches one's entire being. This includes a restoration of the spiritual senses, enabling human beings to enjoy the purpose for which they were created: the glorification of God. St. Bonaventure offers a moving account of the successive recovery of spiritual senses made possible by the work of Christ in *The Soul's Journey into God*:

> When by faith the soul believes in Christ as the uncreated Word and Splendor of the Father, it recovers its spiritual hearing and sight: its hearing to receive the words of Christ and its sight to view the splendors of that Light. When it longs in hope to receive the inspired Word, it recovers through desire and affection the spiritual sense of smell. When it embraces in love the Word incarnate, receiving delight from him and passing over into him through ecstatic love, it recovers its senses of taste and touch.[15]

Bonaventure finds the invigoration of spiritual hearing, sight, smell, taste, and touch to be made possible by the incarnation. The outcome of this

---

14. *Book of Common Prayer* (1979), 285.

15. Bonaventure, *Soul's Journey into God*, 4.3 (p. 89 of the Cousins translation).

is that we can perceive ever more clearly the divine light as we proceed through love toward blissful union with Christ. The movement of the Son into our darkness captivates us, drawing us to share in his resurrection light, thereby restoring our senses and inviting us into eternal joy.

Joy: Which Then Becomes Pure Light

The delight we receive from the Word incarnate, for Bonaventure, is the culmination of the relationship made possible by the work of Christ. To "view the splendors of that Light," we must be drawn into Christ in a grace-enabled process that we will explore in detail in the next chapter. But at this stage it is worth turning attention to a significant event in the biblical accounts of Jesus's life. This experience provided three disciples of Jesus a glimpse of his true glory. After ascending a mountain with their Lord, Peter, James, and John were enabled to see the dazzling radiance of Jesus revealed in his transfiguration (Matt 17:1–8; Mark 9:2–8; Luke 9:28–36). Precisely in the disclosure of the brilliance of the Son's glory, the disciples shared in a foretaste of the eternal joy that awaits all those in Christ. In his reflection on the icon of the transfiguration, David Bentley Hart sees in this moment the expression of the redemption of human nature in the work of the Son:

> And so the icon is at once a revelation of God made man, and of all of us made god in Him. In it, we see how the *kenosis* of the eternal Son—His self-outpouring in the poverty and frailty of infancy, manhood, weariness, sorrow, suffering and death—is also simultaneously our *plerosis*—the filling of our nature with the imperishable splendor of divine beauty and limitless life, the light of rebirth and of resurrection.[16]

Thus in our own account of the christological basis of human hope—that of the bliss of sharing in the divine light—the transfiguration is a natural place to turn.

We might begin by asking what it was that the disciples saw. Was it a transformation of Jesus, or was it rather the revelation of who he always was? Voices from the tradition have tended to favor the latter option, though an interesting exception emerges in Anastasius of Antioch. In his homily on the transfiguration, he suggests that we should think in terms of

---

16. David Bentley Hart, "Foreword," in Nes, *The Uncreated Light*, xiv.

two transfigurations: the kenosis of the incarnation and the transfiguration on the mountain. He writes,

> Once before, Jesus the Savior was transfigured, not before human beings but before his own Father, when "the one who was in the form of God did not consider being equal to God something to cling to, and he emptied himself, taking on the form of a servant" [Phil 2:6–7]. At that time, then, he concealed the divine form, being changed by the form of a servant; but now he restores the form of the servant to its natural appearance—not putting aside the substance of the servant, but making it radiant with divine characteristics.[17]

For Anastasius, it is possible to speak of a transfiguration that occurred in the incarnation, specifically in concealing the divine form in the form of a servant. What happens on the mountain, then, is the radiating of the human body ("the substance of the servant") with the divine glory that rightly and eternally shines in the Son. Even while he is willing to speak of the change occurring in Jesus himself, Anastasius still acknowledges a transformation in the disciples to enable them to recognize what they were seeing. "The Apostles became more clear-sighted," he notes, "since they had been led with Jesus up the mountain." Even more, these apostles had Jesus with them, who "enlightens the guiding core of their intellects, and forms their minds according to his own divine form."[18] On this reading, there is change in both Jesus's human nature and the perceptive capacities of the disciples.

Far more common is an emphasis on the disciples being enabled on the mountain—or, for some commentators, on the ascent of the mountain—to see Jesus as he truly and always is. Leontius of Constantinople speculates that the disciples may have wondered if Christ were simply a human being rather than God in flesh, prompting Jesus's response in the transfiguration: "And that he might divert them from suspicions such as these, he brought them up the mountain, and briefly opened the door of his Incarnation for them, and showed them clearly what great glory was concealed within him."[19] However, Leontius reasons, it was not possible to reveal the full-

17. Anastasius I of Antioch, "On the Transfiguration of Our Lord Jesus Christ," 4, in Daley, *Light on the Mountain*, 135–36.

18. Anastasius I of Antioch, "On the Transfiguration," 5, in Daley, *Light on the Mountain*, 137.

19. Leontius, Presbyter of Constantinople, "Homily for the Transfiguration of Our Lord Jesus Christ," in Daley, *Light on the Mountain*, 126.

ness of the divine radiance to their mortal senses. Therefore, Jesus enabled them to see his identity to the degree that they were able. "For he fulfilled their expectations by showing them the divine glory of his invisible kingly power: not in its full greatness, but as much as those with bodily eyes were able to bear."[20] We encounter a similar instinct in Timothy of Antioch, who suggests that Christ let "the inaccessible beauty of his own divinity appear to them—not in its full greatness, but as much as the unruly eyes of human beings were able to bear."[21] Neither Leontius nor Timothy signal any necessary transformation in the perceptive capacities of Peter, James, and John to be able to see a degree of the Son's divine glory. Rather, they envision the scene as a partial lifting of a sort of covering ("briefly opened the door of his incarnation" for Leontius) that keeps mortal eyes from seeing Jesus's true radiance. And both insist that it is not possible for the disciples, even there on the mountain, to take in the fullness of that glory.

Other interpreters insist that some change has to take place within the disciples to be able to see the light that always shines in the Son. John of Damascus, for example, places the emphasis on the disciples as the locus of transformation: "He was transfigured, then: not taking on what he was not, nor being changed to what he was not, but making what he *was* visible to his own disciples, opening their eyes and enabling them, who had been blind, to see."[22] An even stronger form of this claim appears in Gregory Palamas, who argues that what the disciples see on the mountain is who Jesus always is. They are not seeing a vision of a momentary transformation in Christ, but rather they are granted temporary access to glimpse the boundless radiance that always shines in him: "The light of the Lord's Transfiguration does not come and go, after all, nor is it circumscribed, nor is it subject to our power of perception, even if it is seen by bodily eyes and for a short period of time, and within the narrow space of the mountaintop."[23] This vision required a transformation of their sensory capacities by the Holy Spirit. Gregory continues:

20. Leontius, "Homily for the Transfiguration," in Daley, *Light on the Mountain*, 124.

21. Timothy of Antioch, "Homily on the Cross and the Transfiguration of Our Lord Jesus Christ," in Daley, *Light on the Mountain,* 150.

22. John of Damascus, "Oration on the Transfiguration of Our Lord and Savior Jesus Christ," 12, in Daley, *Light on the Mountain*, 221. Original emphasis.

23. Gregory Palamas, "Homily 34: On the Venerable Transfiguration of Our Lord and God and Savior, Jesus Christ," 8, in Daley, *Light on the Mountain,* 360.

So they saw—in whatever place and degree the power of the divine Spirit bestowed on them—that ineffable light. Those who now do not understand, but blaspheme this light, think that these elect Apostles looked on the light of the transfiguration of the Lord by created powers of perception, and for that reason they attempt to drag down to the creaturely level not only that light, the glory and kingdom of God, but also the power of the Holy Spirit, through which divine things are revealed to the worthy.[24]

To suggest that the three disciples used their regular senses to see the transfigured Jesus, then, is for Gregory an inexcusable error. Such a suggestion would undermine both the ineffability of the divine light and the revelatory agency of the Spirit in the event on the mountain.

If we recall here Bonaventure's account of the restoration of the spiritual senses, it is reasonable to understand the disciples' vision as a preview of what lay ahead for all disciples of Christ. For the physical senses are not equipped to look directly upon the divine glory, which far exceeds the light that radiates through created things. As St. Andrew of Crete observes, "there is nothing, nothing at all, of the things we can contemplate in creation that will grasp the excess of its brilliance!"[25] Even though every created thing shares in the good, Andrew continues, they do not do so in an absolute way. The glimpses of beauty that we are granted in the world are a result of the gracious outpouring of light from God, who is the highest goodness.[26] To take in the primordial light, then, will require a different kind of sensory capacity. The restoration of the spiritual senses enables just that. What the three disciples on the mountain were given, as John of Damascus and Gregory Palamas contend, was a momentary access to this capacity by the work of the Holy Spirit.

One further observation provides an indication of how others might follow Jesus, figuratively speaking, up the mountain to glimpse his radiance. Luke's Gospel in particular notes the immediate context of the transfiguration event. The appearance of Jesus's face and clothing were altered, we read, "as he prayed" (Luke 9:29). For Benedict, this is a significant insight: "The Transfiguration is a prayer event; it displays visibly what happens when Jesus talks with his Father: the profound interpenetration of his

---

24. Gregory Palamas, "Homily 34," 8, in Daley, *Light on the Mountain*, 360.

25. St. Andrew of Crete, "On the Transfiguration of Christ Our Lord," in Daley, *Light on the Mountain*, 194.

26. St. Andrew, "On the Transfiguration," in Daley, *Light on the Mountain*, 194.

being with God, which then becomes pure light. In his oneness with the Father, Jesus is himself 'light from light.' The reality that he is in the deepest core of his being . . . becomes perceptible to the senses at this moment: Jesus's being in the light of God, his own being-light as Son."[27] Two conclusions flow from this observation. First, Jesus's identity is clearly expressed in his prayer life. His union with the Father reflects a sharing in the divine light, and the transfiguration is a revelation to these disciples of who Jesus always is. Second, prayer is shown to be a central means by which human beings can come to share by grace in the divine radiance. What is Christ's by nature becomes ours as a gracious gift: to partake of the feast of eternal light in union with God.

The light that Zechariah and Symeon foresaw in the early chapters of Luke, then, was the divine radiance incarnate. The light of the world that had shone in creation, that was promised as the salvation of Israel and the nations, would now become flesh. In his life, passion, and death, Christ moved ever closer to "those who sit in darkness and in the shadow of death." In his resurrection, the divine light proved victorious over the darkness, "and the darkness did not overcome it." The vision of Peter, James, and John on the mountain was a revelation of Jesus's glory, quite beyond what their unaided physical senses would allow. Their experience at the transfiguration offers a glimpse of the joy that awaits those who, in Christ, will come to share in the eternal feast of light. What happens in them, by grace, to make possible such a gift? In our next chapter, we take up the doctrine of salvation in relation to the divine radiance.

27. Pope Benedict XVI, *Jesus of Nazareth*, I:310.

4

Salvation

"Transformed into the Same Image with Ever-Increasing Glory"

A THEOLOGIAN PREPARING TO embark on the waters of soteriology, the doctrine of salvation, must chart a narrow and tenuous course. On the one hand, the very aim of this area of theology is to explore the nature and effects of the saving work of God with respect to the human being in particular. On the other hand, the temptation toward excessive fascination with the human experience of salvation always lurks—raising the possibility that proper attention to God's action might fade to the background. In this respect soteriological reflection must find its way between the danger of neglecting its task on the one hand and the danger of anthropocentrism on the other. My own Wesleyan tradition has been accused, fairly or unfairly, of the latter on more than one occasion. But here we find considerable promise in reflecting on the way of salvation, the *via salutis*, with an eye to the image of God as light. Doing so enables us to consider the movement of the soul towards God with the primary emphasis on God (the end or *telos*) rather than on the soul that is moving toward the *telos*.

Consider the reflections of the apostle Paul in 2 Corinthians 3. Recounting the glory of God reflecting off of Moses's face in Exodus 34, Paul notes that Moses needed to put a veil over his face. But in Christ, Paul suggests, the veil is set aside. "And all of us, with unveiled faces, seeing the glory of the Lord as though reflected in a mirror, are being transformed into the same image from one degree of glory to another; for this comes from the Lord, the Spirit" (v. 18). Because Christ enables a vision of God's glory "as though reflected in a mirror," we are transformed gradually to reflect the same glory. And Paul insists that this transformation is properly the work of the Holy Spirit; it is not something that we accomplish through our own effort. In this way, Paul is able to account for the difference that is made "when one turns to the Lord" (v. 16), while keeping his primary focus of attention on the glory of the Lord and the transformative agency of the Spirit.

With that image in mind, we might begin to trace the dimensions of our soteriological vision, using the three foci that have guided our reflections throughout this volume. The first aspect, allure, reflects the inclination to respond to glimpses of the sheer beauty of God as those in darkness are attracted to glimpses of light. The second aspect, movement, emerges in three key stages. *Disorientation* calls to mind the confusion that can attend an encounter with God, much as one's eyes need to adjust after stepping quickly into bright sunlight. *Awareness* indicates the new way of seeing everything—including oneself—after one's eyes have adjusted to the light. *Walking in the light* describes the communal and personal way of life that befits a people called by God out of darkness into God's marvelous light. The third aspect of our soteriology of divine light, joy, focuses on the biblical narrative of the transfiguration of Jesus. This Gospel account points us to the ultimate end of human beings—the vision of the radiant God—that entails the infusion of one's own soul with the bliss of God's radiance. We will consider each of these aspects in turn.

Allure: Attraction to the Light

What is it that initiates a soul's movement toward God? A sure starting point is God's own gracious action. This is true both of the divine economy—centered in the life, death, and resurrection of Jesus—and of the work of prevenient grace in the life of each person, together enabling a free response toward God. But what prompts one to begin such a response? At the level of biography, of course, the answers to this question can vary significantly from person to person. For some, it may be the conspicuous sanctity of exemplars in the faith that draws their attention. For others, it may be a crisis event that prompts an openness to the transcendent. For yet others, it may be an encounter with tangible love in a local community of faith, a compelling proclamation of the gospel, or an intellectual case for Christian faith that clears the way for the exercise of the will in the direction of the good.[1] I suspect that for most people, some combination of factors is at work in the early stages of their response to God's grace—particularly for those raised in the Christian faith.

But is there a way theologically to hold these various prompts together, such that neither the necessity of grace nor the free exercise of the graced will is compromised? I would suggest that, in each case, it is the experience of the contrast between God and that which is not God that activates one's inclination for God and moves one to act on it. To be more precise, the encounter with the goodness, beauty, and truth of God, or pointers thereto, draws one to step closer precisely as it manifests the malaise of one's current condition. For some, the appeal of God's goodness may be the dominant factor, while for others dissatisfaction with their present state may be primary. Either way, the contrast between even the potential of life in God and the life they have previously known engages their soul toward movement. In this respect, the notion of attraction can serve as a first facet of our soteriological vision. And biblically speaking, the contrast of light and darkness captures this allure brilliantly.

One important resonance of the image of divine light in Scripture is to signal the attractiveness of God as that which draws our attention. Throughout Isaiah, for example, we see the image of God's light used to represent the hope of a way of life that is different from the darkness of corruption, oppression, and injustice that Israel has known. We might consider Isaiah 9:2: "The people who walked in darkness have seen a great light; those who lived in a land of deep darkness—on them light has shined." Or, similarly, we see in Isaiah 42:16: "I will turn the darkness before them into light, the rough places into level ground. These are the things I will do, and I will not forsake them." While initially these texts appear to use the image of light to convey the *work* of God, the well-known opening of Isaiah 60 (vv. 1–3) makes it clear that this work is not to be separated from the luminous glory of God: "Arise, shine; for your light has come, and the glory of the Lord has risen upon you. For darkness shall cover the earth, and thick darkness the peoples; but the Lord will arise upon you, and his glory will appear over you. Nations shall come to your light, and kings to the brightness of your dawn." The hope reflected in the promise of God's own glory manifested to Israel—and through Israel to the nations—connects the first soteriological dimension to the last (joy, which we shall explore below). The

1. For a very helpful discussion of the relationship between the intellect, the will, and faith, see Gilbey, *We Believe*, 27–30.

grace-enabled movement of the soul toward God begins and ends in the hope of seeing the glory of God, and the entire journey reflects a transition out of darkness.

As we have already seen, it was natural for the early Christian community to connect the incarnation of the Son in Jesus to the manifestation of God's glory using the image of light. Thus the winsome beauty of God attracting people as a light was emphasized in the narration of the life of Jesus. In fact, Matthew cites Isaiah 9:2 (noted above) as a means of introducing Jesus's ministry. Just after recounting that passage with its promise of light that has dawned among those who sat in darkness, Matthew 4:17 notes: "From that time Jesus began to proclaim, 'Repent, for the kingdom of heaven has come near.'" In Matthew's telling, the call Jesus issued to a different way of life was the very means by which the glorious light of God was manifested to the people as a fulfillment of their hope. John's Gospel sounds a similar note, describing the incarnate Word as the light that shines in the darkness (1:5) and citing Jesus's self-identification as "the light of the world," leading those who follow him to the light of life (8:12). This image may help to explain the strange appeal Jesus had to those whom he called in these gospels, such as the calling of Simon and Andrew in Matthew 4:18–20 (immediately after Matthew's allusion to Isaiah 9:2) and the calling of the disciples in the latter part of John 1.

The appeal of the divine light, then, is evident to those who glimpse it from a condition of darkness. While the Isaiah texts frame Israel's hope in terms of a direct vision of God's radiance, other biblical texts suggest that God's radiance can be reflected through creation—typically centered on the locus of the people's worship. When the glory of God returns to the temple in Ezekiel 43, for example, verse 2 notes that "the earth shone with his glory." There is a similar note of particularity in Psalm 50:2, which frames the divine summons to the earth in terms of the beauty of Zion: "Out of Zion, the perfection of beauty, God shines forth." And we saw above how the Gospel writers understood the incarnate Son to mediate that radiance even more directly, in a way that was accessible to those who encountered Jesus. The perception of the contrast between light and darkness, even if limited and mediated, draws one to step toward the beauty of the divine light.

It is important to emphasize that the attractiveness of the light is an attribute of God rather than of the one perceiving—to glimpse something of God is to be drawn to God. Still, there is a corresponding anthropological reality at work. That is, even a limited glimpse of the beauty of God begins to satisfy the natural inclination toward God with which we were created. Pointers to this inclination toward God abound in Christian literature. Perhaps the most famous is found in the opening lines of Augustine's *Confessions*: "You have made us for yourself, and our heart is restless until it rests in you."[2] In a similar vein, the very first question of the Westminster Shorter Catechism connects everlasting joy to our *telos* as human beings: "What is the chief end of man? Man's chief end is to glorify God, and to enjoy him for ever." In the *Catechism of the Catholic Church*, this inclination toward God is grounded in the source and purpose of the creation of human beings: "The desire for God is written in the human heart, because man is created by God and for God; and God never ceases to draw man to himself. Only in God will he find the truth and happiness he never stops searching for."[3] To be drawn to the light of God, therefore, is to begin to experience the fulfillment of our true purpose. Strikingly, Micah 7 takes even the hope of such a glimpse of divine light in the future to be sufficient for repentance. Thus verses 8–9: "Do not rejoice over me, O my enemy; when I fall, I shall rise; when I sit in darkness, the LORD will be a light to me. I must bear the indignation of the LORD, because I have sinned against him, until he takes my side and executes judgment for me. He will bring me out to the light; I shall see his vindication." While that experience initiates a movement toward the end for which we were created, it can be new and disorienting by virtue of its contrast from what we have known. This sense of disorientation leads us to the next aspect of our soteriological vision.

Movement, Part One: Disorientation

Anyone who has stepped out of a dark room into a bright, sunny day outside knows that it takes a moment for one's eyes to adjust to the light. The very presence of light that enables sight can, ironically, blind us temporarily and render a moment of confusion. While this physical experience has everything to do with the way that our eyes work, there is a spiritual parallel with deep roots in the Christian tradition. While the divine light attracts one towards God, it does not immediately bring complete clarity precisely because of the contrast from the life one has previously known. Like with the physical experience of stepping out of darkness into bright sunlight, an initial encounter with the radiance of God can be disorienting. One is

2. Augustine, *Confessions*, I.i (1) (p. 3 in the Chadwick translation).

3. *Catechism of the Catholic Church*, 27.

overwhelmed by the brilliance of the light, and a clearer vision of surrounding realities will come only after a period of adjustment. Some of the most insightful reflections on this experience can be found in the writings of St. Symeon the New Theologian. Indeed, the connection between soteriology and the divine light plays a substantial role in Symeon's theological vision. In giving an account of his own motivation in writing, he points to his firm conviction that the light of God can be experienced by everyone in this present life: "Why am I thus compelled to tell your charity all that God, out of His thirst for our salvation, speaks to us? Simply, in order that through them all you may learn and be persuaded that those who sit in darkness must see the great Light shine, if they only look toward it, and also that none of you may think that though it shone in the past, it is impossible for men of the present day to see it while they are still in the body."[4] Given the centrality of this conviction for Symeon, his work is a useful resource for our soteriological reflections.

In Symeon's accounts of ecstatic experiences of the divine light, the sense of disorientation plays a prominent part. One such account is found in his Sixteenth Catechetical Discourse, and he attributes it to "a young man" who told him the story—though the interpretive tradition has tended to identify this young man with Symeon himself.[5] This account reflects both of the first two facets we are exploring, allure and disorientation:

> I fell prostrate on the ground, and at once I saw, and behold, a great light was immaterially shining on me and seized hold of my whole mind and soul, so that I was struck with amazement at the unexpected marvel and I was, as it were, in ecstasy. Moreover I forgot the place where I stood, who I was, and where, and could only cry out, "Lord, have mercy." . . . It so invigorated and strengthened my limbs and muscles, which had been faint through great weariness, that it seemed to me as though I was stripping myself of the garment of corruption. Besides, there was poured into my soul in unutterable fashion a great spiritual joy and perception and a sweetness surpassing every taste of visible objects, together with a freedom and forgetfulness of all thoughts pertaining to this life. In a marvelous way there was granted to me and revealed to me the manner of the departure from this present life. Thus all the

---

4. Symeon, *Discourses*, XXXIV.12 (p. 357 in the deCatanzaro translation).

5. See Symeon, *Discourses*, 198 n. 1.

perceptions of my mind and my soul were wholly concentrated on the ineffable joy of the Light.[6]

The forgetfulness of his surroundings in this narrative is directly connected to the brilliance of the light, which becomes the sole focus of attention.

A similar dynamic is found in the account of an experience related in Symeon's Twenty-Second Catechetical Discourse, which is attributed to a young man named "George." Again, readers have long suspected that this also was Symeon's own experience, though it is likely a different experience from the one described above.[7] He notes that

> the young man lost all awareness [of his surroundings] and forgot that he was in a house or that he was under a roof. He saw nothing but light all around him and did not know if he was standing on the ground, . . . he was wholly in the presence of immaterial light and seemed to himself to have turned into light. Oblivious of all the world he was filled with tears and with ineffable joy and gladness.[8]

In both instances, the experience of disorientation was joyful and rapturous (this is one place where the analogy with walking into bright sunlight breaks down somewhat). But the brilliant light does not (yet) illuminate the surroundings so that they can be seen more clearly. Rather, the surroundings are not paid any attention because the light is all that matters to the one having the experience.

A couple of points of chronology are in order at this stage. First, Symeon makes it clear that the disorientation that accompanies an experience of the light—he calls it "the rapture of the mind"—is a mark of a beginner on the soul's journey. In his First Ethical Discourse, for example, he reflects on whether the saints will see and know one another in the kingdom of God. Arguing forcefully for the affirmative, Symeon dismisses the objection that the disorientation of ecstasy will render the saints unable to recognize each other in the life to come. Those who make such an objection, he contends, wrongly assume that an initial experience of the divine light in the present life will be the same as the vision of God in the kingdom of God. "They are therefore ignorant of the fact," he writes, "that the rapture of the mind does not apply to the perfect, but to beginners. . . . [One who has arrived

---

6. Symeon, *Discourses*, XVI.3 (pp. 200–201 in the deCatanzaro translation).

7. See Symeon, *Discourses*, 243 n. 1, and Symeon, *Discourses*, 198 n. 1.

8. Symeon, *Discourses*, XXII.4 (pp. 245–46 in the deCatanzaro translation).

suddenly at the vision of the spiritual light] is astonished and, for those who do not also perceive the light, seems like someone who has gone out of his mind. He withdraws his whole intellect into himself in wonder at the vision, at the radiance of Him Who is thus revealed to him."[9] Thus the disorientation Symeon describes is a temporary affair. As one proceeds to adjust one's spiritual senses to the divine light, one "becomes used to the light and lives as if he had always been within it."[10] We will explore the new awareness this brings in connection with the discussion of adjustment below.

A second point of chronology involves the relation between repentance, obedience to God, and the experience of light. While disorientation is, for Symeon, a mark of one who is a "beginner," it is still the case that an initial experience of the divine light requires a particular disposition of the soul. Namely, one must grieve one's sin in humility and keep the commandments of God. When these are present, "then indeed something is opened up in us, like a little hole in the visible roof of the heavens, and the light of the world above, immaterial and spiritual, peeks around it. When the soul perceives this, it enters wholly and completely into ecstasy."[11] At one point, Symeon calls penitence in particular "the gateway that leads out of darkness into light."[12] It is important to note that penitence is not an isolated experience in Symeon's vision; rather, it is an ongoing practice that yields a greater and greater experience of the divine radiance. "When," he writes, "this penitence, this unceasing penitence, is pursued with pain and tribulation until death, it gradually causes us to shed bitter tears and by these wipes away and cleanses the filth and defilement of the soul. Afterwards it produces in us pure penitence and turns the bitter tears into sweet ones. It engenders increasing joy in our hearts and enables us to see the radiance that never sets."[13] There is a progression, then, in Symeon's soteriological vision, but it is not a succession of disconnected and isolated experiences. Rather, it is a progression of increasing joyful apprehension of divine light, enabled by repentance and obedience as a response to divine grace.

9. Symeon, *On the Mystical Life, Vol. 1,* 75–76.

10. Symeon, *On the Mystical Life, Vol. 1,* 78.

11. Symeon, *On the Mystical Life, Vol. 1,* 77.

12. Symeon, *Discourses,* XXVIII.5 (p. 298 in the deCatanzaro translation).

13. Symeon, *Discourses,* IV.16 (pp. 87–88 in the deCatanzaro translation). The theme of tears is a recurring one in Symeon's reflections on repentance. Here he echoes a theme well known in the writings of St. Isaac the Syrian, who also connects the gift of tears to an initial vision of "the light of the age to come". See St. Isaac the Syrian, *Ascetical Homilies,* 201.

The experience of disorientation also appears in a key biblical narrative involving the radiance of God. The transfiguration of Jesus in the Synoptic Gospels is a particularly important signpost for any reflection on divine light. This episode will figure prominently in the reflections on joy below, but it also holds an important indicator of disorientation. When Peter suggests that the disciples build three shelters on the mountain, the Gospel writers hint (and later interpreters state explicitly) that it should be seen as a sign of confusion. In Mark's and Luke's accounts of the transfiguration, Peter's suggestion is followed by an editorial aside that Peter did not know what he was saying (Mark 9:6 and Luke 9:33). The implication is that the brilliance of the light reflecting from Jesus left Peter in a state of disorientation, even as he recognizes that it is "good" for them to be there.

The situation intensifies when, in Matthew's account, the disciples fall down on their faces in terror after hearing the voice of the Father out of the cloud. In a homily on the transfiguration, John Chrysostom reflects on why the disciples fell on their faces at this point. The Matthean text seems to connect it to the voice out of the cloud in particular, but for Chrysostom it was the totality of the experience—including their inability to bear the light—that brought on a sense of anguish: "Why, then, did they fall on their faces on the mountain? Because it was a lonely, high, very quiet place, and his transfiguration inspired terror, and the light was unbearable, and the cloud immense—all of which drove them into deep mental anguish. Amazement came upon them from every side, and they fell down at once in fear and in adoration."[14] Even in this joyous moment of revelation of the divine glory in Jesus, then, the disciples' experience was marked by confusion and holy fear as well as adoration. They would later come to recognize more clearly what had happened on the mountain—and elsewhere on their journey. But such clarity was not to come in that most vivid instance of apprehending the divine radiance.

Movement, Part Two: Awareness

The disorientation of an initial encounter with the divine radiance does not last forever. Rather, it precedes a clearer and fuller way of seeing. This was stated with lucidity by twentieth-century writer A. W. Tozer: "The God of glory sometimes revealed Himself like a sun to warm and bless,

14. John Chrysostom, "Homily 56 on the Gospel of Matthew," in Daley, *Light on the Mountain*, 78.

indeed, but often to astonish, overwhelm, and blind before He healed and bestowed permanent sight."[15] Tozer's image of a temporary blinding followed by a healing of sight is somewhat different from Symeon's image of eyes naturally becoming used to the light—the former emphasizes God's direct healing action while the latter highlights God's creative action in designing spiritual senses to function in a particular way. Still, these accounts hold two things in common. First, the temporary state of disorientation is followed by renewed sight. Second, the transition from disorientation to awareness is attributed primarily to God's action. It is worth noting that the divine light itself was the sole object of focus in the stage of disorientation; now in this stage of awareness, God's restorative action enables one to see what is illuminated by that light.

As we consider precisely what is seen in the renewed vision of divine light, two primary objects come to the fore: a deeper awareness of sin and a clearer path forward toward one's proper end. Regarding the first object, a clearer sense of one's own sin, we might return to Symeon. In a vivid passage in the Seventh Ethical Discourse, he conceives of God as a fire that illumines and purifies the soul. He writes,

> Just so, indeed, does the soul which has begun to burn with divine longing see first of all the murk of the passions within it, billowing out like smoke in the fire of the Holy Spirit. It sees in itself as in a mirror the blackness which accompanies the smoke, and it laments. It senses its evil thoughts like thorns, and its preconceptions, being consumed like dry kindling by the fire and reduced completely to ashes.[16]

It is notable that Symeon envisions the perception of one's sinful condition occurring at the same time as evil thoughts are being consumed by the divine fire. That is, it is the presence of God's purifying action that enables a clearer perception of what needed to be purified. After the purifying action is complete, Symeon suggests that the soul and body also become fire "through participation in the divine and ineffable light."[17]

In describing a clearer perception of sin that attends an experience of divine radiance, Symeon is drawing on a theme with biblical roots. The use of the image of darkness to convey the lack of understanding of one's own sin is a common Pauline device. We can see a representative passage

15. Tozer, *Knowledge of the Holy*, 43.
16. Symeon, *On the Mystical Life, Vol. 2*, 99.
17. Symeon, *On the Mystical Life, Vol. 2*, 99.

in Ephesians 4:18–19: "They [gentiles] are darkened in their understanding, alienated from the life of God because of their ignorance and hardness of heart. They have lost all sensitivity and have abandoned themselves to licentiousness, greedy to practice every kind of impurity." Similar notes are sounded in Romans 1:21 and 2 Corinthians 4:4. Later in Ephesians (in 5:11–14), Christ is envisioned as a light that shines light on the condition of those who have been awakened: "Take no part in the unfruitful works of darkness, but instead expose them. For it is shameful even to mention what such people do secretly; but everything exposed by the light becomes visible, for everything that becomes visible is light. Therefore it says, 'Sleeper, awake! Rise from the dead, and Christ will shine on you.'" Beyond the Pauline corpus, a key text in John's Gospel implies that such exposure is precisely what holds some back from moving toward the light. In that passage, Jesus tells Nicodemus: "And this is the judgment, that the light has come into the world, and people loved darkness rather than light because their deeds were evil. For all who do evil hate the light and do not come to the light, so that their deeds may not be exposed" (John 3:19–20). The suggestion here is that those in darkness are at some level cognizant of the fact that moving toward the light will expose their condition. This aligns with the initial perception of the contrast between light and darkness that we saw in our discussion of attraction. But only those who take those steps come to a true apprehension of their situation in the clarity that emerges after disorientation.

Thankfully, one's own sin is not all that is illumined by the divine light. The second prominent object, a new way forward, becomes immediately visible in the stage of adjustment. If one's awareness of the depth of sin intensifies the longing to move closer toward one's proper end in God, it is the divine radiance that shows the path along which one should move. This is a recurring theme in the Psalter, particularly as the divine light is connected to God's word. We see the following in Psalm 119:105, for example: "Your word is a lamp to my feet and a light to my path." Later in the same Psalm (vv. 128–30): "Truly I direct my steps by all your precepts; I hate every false way. Your decrees are wonderful; therefore my soul keeps them. The unfolding of your words gives light; it imparts understanding to the simple." Psalm 18:27–28 connects humility to the divine light that shows the way out of darkness: "For you deliver a humble people, but the haughty eyes you bring down. It is you who light my lamp; the LORD, my God, lights up my darkness." In both the verses that follow in Psalm 18 and the narrative

placement of this psalm in the story of David in 2 Samuel 22, the emphasis
is on God's saving power in the lives of God's people. Beyond the Psalter,
John 12:35 emphasizes the guidance that Jesus—the visible manifestation
of divine light—provides to his followers. Jesus tells them, "the light is with
you for a little longer. Walk while you have the light, so that the darkness
may not overtake you. If you walk in the darkness, you do not know where
you are going." Precisely as one becomes aware of one's need in the light of
God's revelatory action, one sees the way to the fulfillment of that need by
following the word incarnate.

One of the best-known hymns in the corpus of Charles Wesley, "And
Can It Be That I Should Gain," brings out both dimensions of adjustment
vividly. The key stanza is the fourth:

> Long my imprison'd spirit lay,
> Fast bound in sin and nature's night:
> Thine eye diffus'd a quick'ning ray;
> I woke; the dungeon flam'd with light;
> My chains fell off, my heart was free,
> I rose, went forth, and follow'd thee.[18]

This stanza apparently uses the imagery of Peter's miraculous liberation
from prison in Acts 12 to describe the soul's awakening by divine grace.
(It should be noted that Wesley is not describing *Peter's* spiritual birth with
the imagery of Acts 12, but rather using that narrative of miraculous escape
to describe his own salvation.) It is remarkable that Wesley envisions the
divine ray of light to be the means of his awakening, strongly emphasizing
God's agency in bringing about even the potential of attraction to God. But
upon waking up and taking in his surroundings, the first thing that the
narrator sees illuminated by the divine light is the dungeon in which he is
imprisoned. (Wesley may have had Psalm 107:10-11 in mind here as well:
"Some sat in darkness and in gloom, prisoners in misery and in irons, for
they had rebelled against the words of God, and spurned the counsel of
the Most High.") Thus the awareness of one's own sinful condition is made
particularly clear by the light that enabled the awakening. Yet the narrator
is not left there: once the chains have fallen off and his heart is freed to leave
the prison, the light incarnate (presumably the referent of "thee") shows the
way out of the dungeon. Thus both aspects of adjustment are given narrative expression in this single stanza.

18. The lyrics cited are published under the original title, "Free Grace," in John and
Charles Wesley, *Hymns and Sacred Poems* (1739), 118.

Movement, Part Three: Walking in the Light

With the way now illuminated, Charles Wesley continues: "I rose, went forth, and follow'd thee." This notion of grace-enabled movement toward our ultimate end represents another stage in our soteriological vision. This movement involves the new way of life opened up by the encounter with the divine light. Along this way of life, one experiences the effects of the light precisely as one moves closer to its source. The Johannine language of walking in the light is ideal to designate this movement because it nicely captures three key dimensions: our active response to grace in obedience, the presence of active love in community, and the deepening experience of joy. The theological affirmation that God is light in 1 John 1:5 entails these marks of walking in the light, as reflected in the first two chapters of 1 John. Knowing Jesus—who forgives our sins and enables us to walk in the divine light—is demonstrated by obedience to his commands (2:3). The test of walking in the light is love demonstrated concretely to members of the community (2:9–11). And the effect of walking in the light is the fulfillment of complete joy (1:4).

The active marks of walking in the light do not only appear in Johannine material. Indeed, Pauline texts often connect light with a particular way of life that constitutes the believer's active response to God. If we return to the Ephesians 5 text explored above, for example, we see both general and particular guidelines for living as children of the light. In terms of general signposts, we read that "the fruit of the light is found in all that is good and right and true" (Eph 5:9). This is surrounded by particular examples of the good, right, and true, including one's manner of speech, sobriety, an attitude of thankfulness, the use of time, and a continual pattern of worship (5:3–5, 15–20). A similar note is sounded in 1 Thessalonians 5, where children of the light and of the day are identified by faith, love, sobriety, and the hope of salvation (5:4–11). The point is therefore clear: the divine light is not only something in which we bask passively, but it draws us forward in an active response characterized by particular practices and dispositions.

Another text that uses language of moving into light is 1 Peter 2:9, which identifies God as the one "who called you out of darkness into his marvelous light." In that passage, we see that the way of life that marks the marvelous light of God is not to be walked alone. To be in the light is to be in the community of faith. Indeed, God has called a people into this light for the particular purpose of proclaiming God's salvific deeds: "But you are a chosen race, a royal priesthood, a holy nation, God's own people, in order that you may proclaim the mighty acts of him who called you out of darkness into his marvelous light. Once you were not a people, but now you are God's people; once you had not received mercy, but now you have received mercy" (1 Pet 2:9–10). To walk in the light is a communal act, and the dispositions and practices that reflect this movement are social as well as personal. In a homily on the feast of the transfiguration, the seventh-century writer Anastasius of Sinai connected our own transformation in the likeness of Christ to increasing unity among those in the light: "[Our hope is] that, bathed in a vision of him, flooded with light, we might be changed for the better and joined together as one, and that, grasping hold of the light in light, we might cry out: 'How fearful is this place! This is nothing other than the house of God, this is the gate of heaven!'"[19]

Joy: The Hope of Transfiguration

The reference to complete joy in 1 John 1:4 suggests that our response to God in community orients us to God in a way that enables the fulfillment of our deepest longing. Again, it is assumed that the very ability to manifest these marks of walking in the light is the fruit of divine grace. The connection between holiness and happiness has deep roots in the Christian tradition. Happiness in this sense does not mean a shallow sense of temporary amusement, but rather the fulfillment of the purpose for which one was created. If human beings were created to love, worship, and glorify God, then in that alone will they find ultimate happiness. In this respect, the particular patterns of life that characterize walking in the light draw one toward the fullness of joy. This connection of holiness and happiness was particularly important for John Wesley, who saw the love of God and neighbor as the proper framework to understand and pursue both.[20] Thus the way of life that keeps us in the light of God is the way of happiness.

We might return here to the transfiguration homily of Anastasius, where he continues: "With him, let us also flash like lightning before spiritual eyes, renewed in the shape of our souls and made divine, transformed along with him in order to be like him, always being deified, always

19. Anastasius of Sinai, "Homily on the Transfiguration," in Daley, *Light on the Mountain*, 168.

20. For an analysis of this connection in Wesley's moral theology, see Rebekah L. Miles, "Happiness, Holiness, and the Moral Life in John Wesley," in Maddox and Vickers, *Cambridge Companion to John Wesley*, 207–24.

changing for the better."[21] Like many commentators on the biblical account of the transfiguration, Anastasius takes this event to be a glimpse of what lies ahead for those in Christ. That is, the transfiguration not only reveals the divine glory of Jesus to the three disciples present, but it also reveals the future of all disciples: that in seeing the divine radiance they might be transformed to the point of participating in it. This union with God through Christ, represented by seeing and being illumined by the divine light, is the fulfillment of the attraction to the light that we considered above. Our hope for this union points beyond—even as it gives direction to—earthly life. Indeed, the movement toward the light that characterizes the way of salvation can be conceived as a preparation for eternal participation in that light as our final end.

The connection between the initial apprehension of God's beauty and our immersion in that beauty as characterized by the joy of transfiguration is brought out vividly by John of Damascus. In his Oration on the Transfiguration of Our Lord and Savior Jesus Christ, he suggests that the sheer beauty of the vision makes Peter's desire to remain on the mountain perfectly understandable: "You see this sun—how beautiful and lovely it is, how sweet, how desirable, shining and radiant; you see life—how sweet and desirable it is, how everyone clings to it, how everyone would do anything so as not to throw it away. How much more do you think light in itself, from which all life shines forth, is desirable and sweet?"[22] Understandable though it is, the Damascene warns Peter not to seek divinization before its due time: "Do not look for good things before the time, Peter. The time will come when you will obtain this vision unceasingly."[23] Like Anastasius, John of Damascus sees the transfiguration of Jesus as a preview of the eternal future of those in Christ. Turning his exhortation to his own audience, John writes: "may you always bear in your hearts the loveliness of this vision; may you always hear within you the Father's voice." He immediately makes clear that this means obedience to the particular commandments of Jesus, specifying a number of examples from the Sermon on the Mount. John then continues: "Let us observe these divine commands with total concentration, so that we too may feast upon his divine beauty, and be filled with the taste of his sweetness: now, insofar as this is attainable for those weighed down by this earthly tent of the body; but in the next life more clearly and

21. Anastasius of Sinai, "Homily," in Daley, *Light on the Mountain*, 168.
22. John of Damascus, "Oration," in Daley, *Light on the Mountain*, 225.
23. John of Damascus, "Oration," in Daley, *Light on the Mountain*, 226.

purely, when the 'just shall shine like the sun.'"[24] From the attraction of the light, through the way of obedience that prepares us for the light, to participation in the light itself, John sees a logical movement toward a worthy end.

Given that the foregoing account has focused largely on the transfiguration of Jesus, one might wonder whether the passion, death, and resurrection of Jesus are neglected in a soteriological vision centered on the divine radiance. The answer is clearly negative. The very possibility of participating in the light of God is enabled only by the salvific work of God in Christ manifest in the cross and the empty tomb. In that sense, these reflections on salvation both correspond to and assume all that we explored in chapter 3. Our attention here has been on the effect of God's saving action on humanity, using the image of light to trace the journey. Those who take that journey may be enabled by divine grace to take the words of Psalm 36:9 on their lips and hearts, joining the psalmist in saying to God, "for with you is the fountain of life; in your light we see light."

24. John of Damascus, "Oration," in Daley, *Light on the Mountain*, 229–30.

5

The Holy Spirit

"With the Eyes of Your Heart Enlightened"

WE BEGAN OUR REFLECTIONS on salvation in chapter 4 by exploring 2 Corinthians 3:7–18. As a frame for understanding the transformation of human beings in the light of God, we took up Paul's image of seeing God's glory. Unlike Moses, whose face required a veil after looking upon the divine glory, we are enabled in Christ to look upon that glory with unveiled faces. In doing so, we "are being transformed into the same image from one degree of glory to another." By whose power, then, is such a transformation effected? Paul's response lands squarely in the territory of pneumatology, the doctrine of the Holy Spirit: "for this comes from the Lord, the Spirit" (v. 18). Indeed, the entire passage is cast in terms of "the ministry of the Spirit" (v. 8). The strong pneumatological orientation of this passage cues a fundamental theological point: the change brought about in human beings is most properly attributed to the third person of the Trinity, the Holy Spirit.

It is fitting to affirm, then, that the Holy Spirit is the power by which human beings perceive and then come to share in the divine radiance. But our guiding task presses us to ask a further question: in what ways might the image of light relate directly to the Spirit? How might we understand the Holy Spirit *as* light? The answer is not as clear as we might initially suppose, particularly given the prevalence of light for depicting the Spirit in Christian art.[1] Gerald O'Collins notes, for example, that New Testament

---

1. One thinks, for example, of the dove bathed in light in scenes of the Annunciation (Philippe de Champaigne, Bartolomé Esteban Murillo, Francesco Albani) or in El Greco's *The Holy Trinity*.

links between the Holy Spirit and life and truth are rather common. Yet "direct links of the Holy Spirit with 'glory' and 'light' are less apparent."[2] While there is minimal biblical material that makes an explicit connection between the Spirit and light, O'Collins points out that the link does get picked up by a handful of figures in the Christian tradition.[3] Most typically, the Spirit is connected with light or radiance in accounts of the Trinity, particularly when the sun is used as a trinitarian image.

In what follows, we want to develop the connection between radiance and pneumatology by means of the threefold pattern we have used throughout the book. We face an intriguing challenge in the first section on allure. For while the brilliance of the divine light naturally draws the gaze of creatures, the third person of the Trinity does not seek to become the focal point of that attention. Rather, the Spirit points continually to Christ, who reveals the Father as the radiance of God's glory. Therefore, our discussion of allure will emphasize the Spirit's role as the means of our attraction to the divine light rather than as the direct object of that attraction. To this end, we will focus on the role of the Spirit in the life and ministry of Jesus, and then we will consider the Spirit's role in the illumination of Scripture. Our second progression, on movement, will take up the one prominent biblical image of the Spirit that relates directly to radiance: the image of fire. As one might expect, the account of Pentecost will be central to our reflections on the Spirit's work of transformation and empowering mission. Our third and final section, on joy, will take up the radiance of the Holy Spirit as reflected in the lives of sanctified human beings. The movement initiated by the Spirit's fire at Pentecost draws us toward the joy of sharing in the divine light. The patristic image of the sun, particularly of the Spirit as the radiance of the object illuminated by the divine ray, will prove helpful to our purposes here. The path to such joy is not an easy one, of course. As 1 Peter 4 reminds us, by sharing in the suffering of Christ, we also delight when his glory is revealed (v. 13). And those who face such trials are blessed, "because the spirit of glory, which is the Spirit of God, is resting on" them (v. 14).

2. Gerald O'Collins, S.J., "Light from Light," in O'Collins and Meyers, *Light from Light*, 113.

3. O'Collins, "Light from Light," in O'Collins and Meyers, *Light from Light*, 118–20.

Allure: Pointing to the Risen Christ

In his book *The Orthodox Way*, Bishop Kallistos Ware notes that there is a quality of elusiveness to the Holy Spirit. This quality is captured by some of the biblical imagery for the Spirit, such as wind and fire.[4] Ware also suggests that there is something in the distinct mission of the Spirit that reflects this elusiveness; namely, the Holy Spirit's role in connecting us to Christ. "The Holy Spirit, then, does not speak to us about himself, but he speaks to us about Christ," Ware contends. "Herein lies the reason for the anonymity or, more exactly, the transparency of the Holy Spirit: he points, not to himself, but to the risen Christ."[5] To be sure, the Spirit draws us toward the allure of the divine light. But the aim of the particular mission of the third person is to orient us to the second person, the Son incarnate. The Holy Spirit draws us toward Jesus, the light of the world, who reflects the radiance of God the Father.

If the Holy Spirit points us *toward* the light, then, is it possible to speak of the Spirit *as* light? The classical doctrine of appropriation prompts us to answer in the affirmative. This doctrine holds that every act of the triune God *ad extra* is shared by all three persons. This notion does not preclude the identification (or, better, appropriation) of particular missions of the Son and the Spirit. Rather, it reminds us that their distinct operations in the economy of salvation are ultimately shared actions of the indivisible Triune God. Thus it was the Son, not the Father or the Spirit, who took on human nature in the incarnation. But the Father and the Spirit are, so to speak, involved in the incarnation of the Son at every moment. The light that shines in and through the incarnate Son is the divine light of the Holy Trinity. As we saw in chapter 1, it is proper to identify the Father as the source of this light. But it is precisely because the Spirit shares in this light eternally that we can be oriented toward the incarnate light of the Son by the Spirit's work. As like recognizes like, the Holy Spirit moves within us to draw us to the light of the world.

In chapter 3, we explored a number of ways the Gospels—particularly Luke and John—engage the symbol of light in their accounts of Jesus's life and ministry. While both Luke and John (together with Luke's companion volume Acts) allude to the power of the Holy Spirit that would come upon believers after Jesus's ascension, the Spirit is also significantly involved in

4. Ware, *The Orthodox Way*, 90–91.
5. Ware, *The Orthodox Way*, 94.

the ministry of Jesus. It would be too much to say that the filling of Jesus with the Holy Spirit makes Jesus the light of the world; that is secured in the incarnation of the Word, who is eternally divine light. But we can affirm that the Spirit's empowerment of Jesus's ministry begins to reveal that light publicly in and through Jesus.[6] In Luke, for example, we noted how the prophesies of Zechariah and Simeon looked ahead to the salvation that Jesus would bring as a light to the world. It is significant, then, that the Holy Spirit is prominent in the account of the beginning of Jesus's public ministry in Luke 3 and 4. The Spirit descends on Jesus in his baptism (3:21–22), leads Jesus (who is "full of the Spirit") into the wilderness (4:1–2), and empowers Jesus as he begins teaching in Galilee (4:14–15). Further, in prayer, Jesus rejoices "in the Holy Spirit" in Luke 10:21. It is in the Holy Spirit, then, that the dawn foreseen by Zechariah begins to break upon the world and "give light to those who sit in darkness and in the shadow of death" (Luke 1:78–79).

A similar pattern emerges in the Gospel of John, which frames the story of Jesus as "the true light, which enlightens everyone," who "was coming into the world" (1:9). When Jesus makes his first appearance, John the Baptist testifies that he saw "the Spirit descending from heaven like a dove, and it remained on him" (1:32). John the Baptist also reveals that the one who sent him had prepared him for this vision, and that the one on whom the Spirit remained "is the one who baptizes with the Holy Spirit" (1:33). Then in Jesus's conversation with Nicodemus in chapter 3, Jesus claims that he speaks divine words precisely because of his connection to the Spirit: "He whom God has sent speaks the words of God, for he gives the Spirit without measure" (3:34). In both Luke and John, then, we see the ways that the Holy Spirit reveals the light of the world—which Jesus always was and is—through Jesus's baptism and public ministry.

If the Spirit's activity in Jesus's ministry shines his eternal divine light to the world, then these same Gospels also attest that this work continues after Jesus's ascension. The Spirit descends on Jesus and fills him with power, and Jesus then reveals to the disciples that the Spirit will come upon

---

6. With regard to the emergence of a great deal of recent work on Spirit christology, I would contend that each proposal should be evaluated carefully on merit in light of the witness of Scripture and the Christian tradition. I would simply add that such approaches to christology might best be regarded as a complement to, rather than a substitute for, Logos christology. We should rightly be hesitant about any proposals to replace the concept of the Logos outright, particularly given its prominence in the Johannine and patristic traditions.

them to guide and empower them. We can detect here a shift in the primary locus of the Holy Spirit's activity from the incarnate Son to the community of disciples—without for a moment limiting the freedom of the Spirit to move anywhere at any time. One could thus say that the Holy Spirit who radiated the divine light outward through the ministry of Jesus now works in and through people to perceive and respond to the light of the world. At the end of Luke's Gospel, Jesus alludes to the coming power of the Spirit in his words to the disciples just before his ascension: "And see, I am sending upon you what my Father promised; so stay here in the city until you have been clothed with power from on high" (24:49). Luke picks up this theme again at the beginning of Acts, now explicitly connecting the coming power to the Holy Spirit. In the period between his resurrection and ascension, Jesus tells the disciples that they will be "baptized with the Holy Spirit" (Acts 1:5) and that they would "receive power when the Holy Spirit has come upon" them (1:8). This promise is fulfilled in the Pentecost narrative in Acts 2, to which we will return below. Throughout Acts, the Holy Spirit fills and empowers believers to serve as witnesses to Christ's redemptive work.[7] It is worth noting that, near the end of Acts, Paul turns to the image of light in describing his Spirit-empowered work to King Agrippa. After recounting his conversion—in which the risen and ascended Jesus appeared to him by means of a bright light (26:13)—Paul recalls how Jesus called him to the gentiles "to open their eyes so that they may turn from darkness to light and from the power of Satan to God, so that they may receive forgiveness of sins and a place among those who are sanctified by faith in" Jesus (26:18). He continues by insisting that he has proclaimed nothing but what the prophets and Moses foretold, that the Messiah would suffer and that "by being the first to rise from the dead, he would proclaim light both to our people and to the Gentiles" (26:22–23). In this way, Luke brings his two-volume account full circle with the fulfillment of the prophecies of Zechariah and Simeon at the beginning of his Gospel.

John's Gospel also anticipates the Holy Spirit's guidance and empowerment of the disciples after Jesus's ascension. Throughout his teaching ministry, Jesus repeatedly identified the Spirit as central to the new life promised to his disciples. He names the Spirit as the source of new birth (John 3:5–8), life (6:63), and living water (7:38–39). One could make a strong case for a pneumatological reading of Jesus's teaching about worship

7. For just a sampling of such references, we might point to Acts 4:8; 7:55; 8:29; 10:19; 13:2; 19:6, 21.

in his conversation with the Samaritan woman: "God is spirit, and those who worship him must worship in spirit and truth" (4:24).[8] The anticipation of the Holy Spirit intensifies in Jesus's farewell discourse of John 14–17. Jesus tells the disciples that the Father will send an advocate, "the Spirit of truth," who will abide with them and will be with them forever (14:16–17). In verse 26, that advocate is named specifically as the Holy Spirit, who will teach the disciples everything and remind them of all Jesus has said to them. The coming advocate will "testify on behalf" of Jesus, just as the disciples are called to do as well (15:26-27). Later in the discourse, in chapter 16, we learn more about the activity of the coming Spirit: the advocate will "prove the world wrong about sin and righteousness and judgment" (v. 8–11), will guide the disciples into all truth (v. 13), and will glorify Jesus, because he will take what is Jesus's and declare it to the disciples (v. 14). The point is clear: the Holy Spirit will continue to radiate the divine light to the community of faith. The Father is the source of this light, the incarnate Son is the visible expression of the light, and the Spirit enables the disciples to perceive it continually.

Jesus promised that the Holy Spirit would guide the community of faith into all truth. One mode of this guidance that has been recognized by many voices in the Christian tradition is the illumination of the Spirit in our reading of Scripture. On such an account, the Spirit works within our cognitive faculties to perceive God's Word in the words of the Bible. (We should be careful to distinguish this more limited focus on the biblical text from a broader account of illumination in which divine assistance is needed in ordinary cognitive operations, such as we find in Augustine.[9] The latter is a much more contested concept in the Christian tradition.) Two key texts provide biblical grounding of the illumination of Scripture. The first is Psalm 119, a prayer of delight in God's law. Verse 18 appeals to the Lord's agency in enabling us to take in these words: "Open my eyes, so that I may behold wondrous things out of your law." Later in this lengthy

8. One must always be careful to distinguish between the claim that the Triune God is spirit—that is, that God is not corporeal—and references to the Spirit, the third person of the Trinity. While the former appears dominant in the first clause of John 4:24, the latter is a very sensible reading of the final clause.

9. For just one example, see Augustine, *Confessions*, IV.xv.25. While Augustine did not reject the notion of the Spirit's illumination in our interpretation of Scripture, he was critical of simplistic accounts of that notion. He was particularly suspicious of claims to illumination that evaded the crucial place of rules of interpretation in the community of faith. See Augustine, *On Christian Doctrine*, preface: 8.

psalm, we see the image of light used to describe this process of opening the Scriptures. "The unfolding of your words," reads verse 130, "gives light." The other biblical text, 1 Corinthians 2, emphasizes the role of the Holy Spirit in unfolding the divine word. We are unable to perceive the things of God by means of our ordinary capacities. But "we have received," Paul contends, "the Spirit that is from God, so that we may understand the gifts bestowed on us by God" (v. 12). By contrast, those who have not received the gifts of God's Spirit "are unable to discern them because they are spiritually discerned" (v. 14). Because the things of God can only be perceived in their depth by God, we need the light of the Holy Spirit to guide us into such knowledge as we can attain.

This vision of the illumination of the Holy Spirit has been a particular point of emphasis in the Reformed tradition (though certainly not exclusively there).[10] For example, John Calvin offered a particularly sharp articulation of the Spirit's role in receiving Scripture in Book I of his *Institutes of the Christian Religion*:

> For as God alone can properly bear witness to his own words, so these words will not obtain full credit in the hearts of men, until they are sealed by the inward testimony of the Spirit. The same Spirit, therefore, who spoke by the mouth of the prophets, must penetrate our hearts, in order to convince us that they faithfully delivered the message with which they were divinely entrusted.[11]

The necessity of the Spirit penetrating our hearts is no doubt related to Calvin's deep sense of the epistemic consequences of sin. Yet the primary appeal here is to human finitude, as Calvin echoes the 1 Corinthians 2 text, and particularly verse 11: "no one comprehends what is truly God's except the Spirit of God." We see the Spirit's work in unfolding Scripture explicitly connected to the image of light in the Westminster Confession of Faith: "we acknowledge the inward illumination of the Spirit of God to be necessary for the saving understanding of such things as are revealed in the Word."[12] Yet again, the work of the Holy Spirit in guiding the community of disciples into all truth is envisioned as a reflection of the divine radiance.

---

10. St. Symeon the New Theologian, for example, has a strong doctrine of the illumination of the Spirit. An especially clear instance is found in *Discourses*, XXVIII.3 (p. 297 in the deCatanzaro translation).

11. Calvin, *Institutes*, I.7.4 (p. 33 in the Beveridge translation).

12. *The Westminster Confession of Faith*, I.VI.

The allure of the incarnate Word thus reflects two realities: the revelation of the divine light in Christ and the Spirit's work of radiating that light to the eyes of our heart. And as we have seen, that work of the Spirit continues in and through the community of faith across time and space. Even after the ascension of Jesus, the light of the world continues to shine so that mortal eyes can perceive the glory of God. And this is because the Holy Spirit continues, as Ware put it, to point to Christ. When the allure of the divine radiance captivates us, what then? We not only perceive the light of God in the Spirit; we are also drawn by the Spirit to participate in it. But as we saw in the last chapter, such participation requires transformation. There must be a process of refining for sinful creatures to move deeper into communion with God. That which cannot remain in the presence of God must be left behind, so that what remains conforms to the image of Christ. And by what other means could this happen than by fire?

Movement: Kindled into a Living Flame

We noted above both the Lukan and the Johannine accounts of Jesus's promise of the coming Holy Spirit to the disciples. In Luke and Acts in particular, the promise was focused on the power from on high that would come upon them. That promise was fulfilled in the Pentecost scene narrated in Acts 2. Most significant for our purposes is the visual marker of the Holy Spirit's presence in that scene, which we find in verse 3: "Divided tongues, as of fire, appeared among them, and a tongue rested on each of them." There appears to have been something of a challenge in conveying just what was seen resting on each disciple, reflecting the novelty of the situation. The reference to "tongues" here is likely a reference to the shape of what was seen, like the shape a flame.[13] Yet the appearance of fire in this narrative does sound an echo of a text from the Gospel of Luke. In Luke 12:49, Jesus issued a declaration that was as cryptic as it was provocative: "I came to bring fire to the earth, and how I wish it were already kindled!" Now in light of the Pentecost narrative, we are able to read Jesus's claim as an allusion to the work of the coming Holy Spirit.

The image of the Holy Spirit as fire points us in two important directions. The first is the work of the Spirit in empowering the community of disciples for ministry. Just as fire spreads quickly, so also the Holy Spirit

---

13. So C. K. Barrett in *Acts*, 18. Barrett also finds the occurrence of equivocal uses of "tongues" in verses 3 and 4 to be surprising.

moved through the ministry of the apostles to spread throughout the region. To be sure, this is the dominant emphasis in Acts. The second direction in which the sign points us is the refining function of fire. Just as fire melts away impurities, so also the Spirit sanctifies believers by removing that which cannot bear the light of God. And it is necessary that these operations of the Holy Spirit function together, if the disciples were to witness to Jesus by both word and deed. The sign of transformed lives is an important means of witness, as attested by Paul in his speech before Agrippa in Acts 26. So the fire of the Spirit that spread in and through the church's witness was the fire that sanctified those who were captivated by that witness. Let us explore these dimensions in turn.

The dramatic fulfillment of Jesus's promise of the Spirit inaugurates a new chapter in the mission of the community of disciples. As the Spirit continues to radiate the light of the world, the church is empowered by the same Spirit to serve as witnesses to that light. Ivan Satyavrata suggests that this connection between Pentecost and mission is vital to the identity of the church: "The Holy Spirit played a crucial role in every aspect of the kingdom mission of Jesus. At Pentecost the Spirit came on the early church in power so Jesus's mission could be advanced and completed. There is thus an indissoluble relationship between Pentecost and the missionary witness of the church."[14] It is notable in this regard that Jesus had instructed his disciples to wait in Jerusalem for the fulfillment of the promise of the Spirit (Acts 1:4–5). Rather than immediately sending them off on their mission of witness, he commanded them to remain where they were. The primary mark of their life together during this brief interval between the ascension and Pentecost was prayer (Acts 1:14). And it was in the context of this devotion to prayer that the Holy Spirit came upon them in power. This signals not only the need for divine empowerment to carry out their work of witness, but also the posture in which they would receive and remain in the Spirit's presence: attentiveness to God in prayer.

But why is the Spirit marked visually by fire in this instance? One intriguing suggestion is offered by Eugene F. Rogers Jr., who suggests that the emergence of fire in this scene is significant in marking out this particular community and these particular disciples for that task. He argues that the tongues of fire "perform the witness's deictic work of pointing out and marking. For this reason fire becomes one of the chief hallmarks of

14. Satyavrata, *The Holy Spirit*, 121.

the Spirit's witness, the witness to the witness as it were."[15] The disciples had been called, in Acts 1:8, to serve as witnesses to Jesus in expanding geographical contexts. In this respect, Rogers contends that the presence and work of the Spirit would be a key sign in the reception of the disciples' witness across various regions. So the Holy Spirit witnesses to the disciples, in this case visually by fire, and the disciples now empowered will witness to Jesus. With this in mind, fire is a fitting sign indeed. If we conceive of fire as an instance of light spreading, then the Spirit's movement outward through the community of disciples represents the spreading of the divine light in the world. The Holy Spirit is the divine light that points to the divine light of the world, the Son, now through the community that spreads as fire.

There is also an element of reception involved on the part of the disciples in living into their missionary calling. The power of the Spirit is necessary to fulfill this task, but they also must welcome this power—which is not at all a given. While fire gives light and heat, it is also unsettling. The capacity to unnerve those around it is one of the inescapable features of the image of fire. In this regard, the sheer strangeness and power of the coming of the Spirit at Pentecost called forth either reverence or apprehension. Beth Felker Jones notes that this dynamic always entails a choice for those in the presence of that power:

> Here is the presence of the Spirit, visible to the church and to the world, in terrifying power. . . . The wild power of the Spirit's work at Pentecost and subsequently in the church has always been interpreted in at least two ways. This power can be embraced, perhaps even ecstatically, with a deep confidence in the Spirit's work, or this power can be rejected and denied.[16]

Jones suggests that this choice continues in every age and in every person as the Spirit-empowered mission of the church moves forward. To accept the calling as witnesses and receive the power that will enable its fulfillment, the community of disciples must welcome the Holy Spirit's presence and movement in reverence.

When believers welcome the Spirit's work through them, they also welcome the Spirit's work within them. This leads us to our second dimension of fire; namely, its purifying capacity. The arrival of the Holy Spirit at Pentecost initiated a movement that resulted in changed lives. The pattern of the Spirit's work of transformation varies throughout Acts. We find

15. Rogers, *After the Spirit*, 205.
16. Jones, *God the Spirit*, 90.

dramatic conversions, such as Saul (Acts 9:1–22) and the jailor at Philippi (16:25–34). We also see people who are earnestly seeking God connect with the community of disciples, eventually resulting in their baptism (the Ethiopian official in 8:26–40, Cornelius in 10:1–48, Lydia in 16:13–15). In the Cornelius narrative, we also find an example of the Holy Spirit's transformative work within someone who is already a believer. The voice that began to expand Peter's understanding of the scope of God's salvation is directly attributed to the Spirit in Acts 10:19. When the same Spirit comes upon the gentiles who heard Peter's message, the astonishment of the circumcised believers who are with Peter reflects further transformation within the community (10:45). The fire of the Holy Spirit refines the disciples as it spreads and expands their number.

The image of the Holy Spirit as fire was taken up in two notable hymns of Charles Wesley, both with the same title: "Come, Holy Ghost, All-Quick'ning Fire." Both of these hymns highlight the second dimension of the Spirit's work that we have been emphasizing, with a primary focus on sanctification. After addressing the Spirit as fire, the first of these hymns takes up the theme of divine light in articulating the goal of sanctification:

> Thy witness with my spirit bear,
> That God, *my* God, inhabits there,
> Thou, with the Father and the Son,
> Eternal light's coeval beam.
> Be Christ in me, and I in him,
> 'Till perfect we are made in one.[17]

Having identified the characteristically Wesleyan goal of Christian perfection, the next stanza acknowledges that there is still a long way to go before that work of the Spirit is complete:

> When wilt thou my whole heart subdue?
> Come, my Lord, and form my soul a-new,
> Emptied of pride, and self, and hell.

In a later stanza, Wesley returns to the image of light. Drawing on the language of Psalm 36:9, he emphasizes the Holy Spirit's work of aligning the human will with the divine will as central to sanctification:

> My will be swallow'd up in thee:
> Light in thy light still may I see,
> Beholding thee with open face.

17. Charles Wesley, "Come, Holy Ghost, All-Quick'ning Fire," in John and Charles Wesley, *Hymns and Sacred Poems* (1740), 45–46. Original emphasis.

The hymn concludes with an appeal to feel and know, as the result of the Spirit's witness, "that I am one with God." Thus the Holy Spirit's sanctifying work ultimately results, for Wesley, in a direct experience of union with God.

Wesley's second hymn of that same title begins with an emphasis on the theme of human longing for God. The first two stanzas describe how the experience of the Spirit's presence, in response to a desire for the Spirit, brings forth an even greater desire for more. The remaining stanzas draw out the Holy Spirit's preparation of the heart to be a fitting dwelling place of the divine. This preparatory agency includes bringing peace, life, and comfort in the present, witnessing to one's status as a child of God, engraving pardon in Christ on the heart, and being present as an "earnest of love" and a "pledge of heav'n." The final stanza offers an apt summary of the hymn:

> Come, Holy Ghost, all-quick'ning fire,
> Come, and in me delight to rest!
> Drawn by the lure of strong desire,
> O come and consecrate my breast:
> The temple of my soul prepare,
> And fix thy sacred presence there![18]

The Holy Spirit, envisioned as the fire of Pentecost, both ignites our desire for God's indwelling and makes the human soul a fitting space to receive it.

It is important to remember that sanctification is connected to the mission of the Son in the incarnation. As we saw above, the Holy Spirit points to Christ and connects people with the work of Christ. In this respect, the teaching ministry of Jesus as witnessed by the Gospel narratives becomes an important means of the Spirit's sanctifying activity. Servais Pinckaers draws on the image of illumination, for example, to describe the process of refining sinful human beings through Jesus's Sermon on the Mount: "We all need the grace of Christ in order to be healed of the sins which the Sermon on the Mount reveals to us as would a mirror held aloft and reflecting the penetrating light of the Holy Spirit."[19] The picture that Pinckaers draws is striking—the light of the Spirit reflects off of the teaching of Christ to unveil and remove the sin that keeps us from sharing in that light. The grace of Christ is mediated through his words in the Sermon, and we are connected to that transformative grace through the Spirit's illuminating action.

18. Charles Wesley, "Come, Holy Ghost, All-Quick'ning Fire," in John and Charles Wesley, *Hymns and Sacred Poems* (1739), 184–85.

19. Pinckaers, *The Pursuit of Happiness*, 20–21.

The sanctifying movement of the Spirit, once again, is to be welcomed by those captivated by the divine light. And this must be an active welcoming if that transformative work is to be completed. This is not because God cannot work without our active reception, but rather because God will not work without our active reception. If God's purpose in creation was love, that we might freely be enabled to share in the bliss of eternal divine light, then the mode of God's redemption must be invitation rather than compulsion. Ware suggests that as we respond to that invitation actively, the flame of the Holy Spirit within us is fanned:

> Unless we co-operate with God's grace—unless, through the exercise of our free will, we struggle to perform the commandments—it is likely that the Spirit's presence within us will remain hidden and unconscious. As pilgrims on the Way, then, it is our purpose to advance from the stage where the grace of the Spirit is present and active within us in a hidden way, to the point of *conscious awareness*, when we know the Spirit's power openly, directly, with the full perception of our heart. . . . The Pentecostal spark of the Spirit, existing in each one of us from Baptism, is to be kindled into a living flame.[20]

The suggestion that the fire of the Spirit can be ignited within us points us in an important new direction: by God's grace, we can be bearers of the divine light. The Holy Spirit radiates the light of the world, Christ incarnate, to our minds and hearts. But the Spirit also burns within, preparing us to reflect that light. The idea that the transfiguration of Jesus gives us a glimpse of our own eternal participation in the divine light, which we explored in the last chapter, now takes further shape. It is the action of the Holy Spirit that makes such participation possible. This pneumatological observation makes it clear why joy is one of the fruits of the Spirit (Gal 5:22). If the work of the Spirit moves us toward union with the God who is light, we will be moving toward the eternal happiness for which we were created.

Joy: Which Lights Us and Is Enjoyed by Us

It is helpful at this stage to return to some of the patristic reflections on the divine light that we explored in chapter 1, particularly as they relate to the Holy Trinity. We recall the observations of Gregory of Nazianzus and Athanasius that it is in the Spirit that we perceive the divine light, a move

20. Ware, *The Orthodox Way*, 100. Original emphasis.

that we traced through the Gospel accounts above. Even more pronounced is John of Damascus's use of the image of the sun to envision the work of the Spirit in relation to the other persons of the Trinity. We noted how the Damascene conceived of the Father in terms of the sun itself, the source of light, and the Son as the rays of the sun making that light visible to us. He then used the image of the brightness or radiance reflecting off of us in reference to the Holy Spirit. "For the sun [the Father] is the source of its rays [the Son] and brightness [the Spirit]," he wrote, "and the brightness is communicated to us through the rays, and that it is which lights us and is enjoyed by us."[21] The phrase "which lights us and is enjoyed by us" captures pneumatologically the human experience of the Spirit's work within. The agent who makes the divine light shine in us is the third person of the Trinity, such that the radiance both immerses us in joy and reflects off of us. It is fitting here that the sun calls to our minds both light and fire, as both dimensions of the fire imagery are reflected in the language used by John of Damascus. The brightness of the divine light that the Spirit shines upon us is conducive to the church's mission of witness, as we saw in the image of fire spreading. And the joy of basking in that light is the outcome of the Spirit's refining work of sanctification that enables union with God.

The bliss of experiencing the divine light was expressed vividly by St. Symeon the New Theologian, whose testimony we examined at length in chapter 4. Here we must consider a crucial addition to those reflections by noting the thoroughly pneumatological character of Symeon's theological vision. He is consistent in identifying the presence and action of the Holy Spirit as the source of our participation in the radiance of God. Yves Congar put this point concisely: "For Symeon, the Holy Spirit is the principle of all spiritual life."[22] The remarkable ecstatic experiences that Symeon reported were fostered in and by the Holy Spirit. It is significant for our purposes, then, that Symeon connected the Holy Spirit with light. Congar again goes straight to the heart of the matter: "The Spirit is light. Symeon's mystical experience was above all an experience of light and an experience of the Spirit."[23] As a sample of a consistent pattern throughout Symeon's work, we might point to a few examples from his Discourses. The connection between sanctification and the luminous vision of God is grounded

21. John of Damascus, An Exact Exposition of the Orthodox Faith, I.8 (p. 188 in the Chase translation).

22. Congar, I Believe in the Holy Spirit, I:94.

23. Congar, I Believe in the Holy Spirit, I:96.

pneumatologically in the following passage: "Thou Thyself becamest visible when Thou, by the clear light of the Holy Ghost, hadst entirely cleansed my mind."[24] Symeon also links insight into the mysteries of God to our experience of the divine light, which is the direct work of the Holy Spirit: "Where there is the enlightenment of the Spirit there is the outpouring of the light of God, there is God in the wisdom and knowledge of His mysteries."[25] Finally, in outlining the qualifications of a worthy candidate for pastoral office, Symeon draws together many of the themes we have explored in this chapter: "you must see in yourself the abundant grace of the Holy Spirit enlightening the interior of your heart and making it into a very sun, and clearly experience the miracle of the bush taking place within you, so that you are inflamed by union with the unapproachable fire, yet not consumed thereby because your soul is set free from all passion."[26] Symeon's alludes, of course, to Moses's encounter with the burning bush in Exodus 3. This biblical echo is directed toward a very specific purpose: to help the reader recognize the Spirit's work of sanctification as the means to the end of union with God.

There is another notable biblical allusion in the last passage from Symeon. The language of "the abundant grace of the Holy Spirit enlightening the interior of your heart" calls to mind Ephesians 1:17–19, a text that provides a fitting conclusion to our reflections in this chapter. That passage articulates a prayer for the saints at Ephesus:

> I pray that the God of our Lord Jesus Christ, the Father of glory, may give you a spirit of wisdom and revelation as you come to know him, so that, with the eyes of your heart enlightened, you may know what is the hope to which he has called you, what are the riches of his glorious inheritance among the saints, and what is the immeasurable greatness of his power for us who believe, according to the working of his great power.

Whether or not the phrase "a spirit of wisdom and revelation" is taken as a direct reference to the Holy Spirit, the plea is thoroughly pneumatological. The divine activity of guiding the community of faith into knowledge of God is properly appropriated to the Holy Spirit. The image selected for this revelatory experience is vivid: the enlightening of the eyes of the heart. In that remarkable phrase, the presence of a spiritual sense of sight is

24. Symeon, *Discourses,* XXXVI.10 (p. 374 in the deCatanzaro translation).

25. Symeon, *Discourses,* II.8 (p. 53 in the deCatanzaro translation).

26. Symeon, *Discourses,* XVIII.11 (p. 217 in the deCatanzaro translation).

presumed, but so is the need for that sense to be activated by the illumination of the Spirit.

Once operative, the eyes of the heart are able to see what can only be perceived in the Spirit's light: hope, the riches of God's inheritance among believers, and divine power. These three objects of spiritual sight are related to each other. The hope of believers in the present is rooted in the power of God that was manifested in the resurrection (v. 20). The reference to the riches of God's inheritance calls back to verses 3–14, a passage that identifies the content of our hope: the forgiveness of sins (v. 7), adoption as children of God through Jesus (v. 5), and the divine plan to gather all things up in Christ (v. 10). God's power to bring this plan to fruition gives believers hope of what awaits: "that we might live for the praise of his glory" (v. 12).

The light of the Holy Spirit, therefore, enables the eyes of our heart to perceive the eternal joy that awaits those who have become children of God through Christ. And the presence of this hope means that we are able to share in this joy even now. This is why the passage is framed in terms of repeated affirmations of beatitude: "Blessed be the God and Father of our Lord Jesus Christ, who has blessed us in Christ with every spiritual blessing in the heavenly places" (v. 3). The bliss of basking in the divine light is made possible by the redemptive work of the Son, the light of the world, and we are enabled both to share in and perceive that hope by the light of the Holy Spirit. It should not escape our notice that Ephesians 1 is marked by repeated plural pronouns, both first person and second person, as well as by the repeated use of a key plural noun: the saints. The implication of this observation is reinforced by the reference to the church as the body of Christ in verses 22–23. That is, the joyful hope perceived by the eyes of the heart is a shared hope. The Spirit that illuminates this vision is at work in the community of faith, prompting love and mutual prayer among the saints (v. 15–16). To be drawn to the light of God is to be drawn into communion with fellow adopted children of God, so to the church we now turn.

6

Church

*"The People Who Sat in Darkness
Have Seen a Great Light"*

IN A PASSAGE FROM Book X of his *Confessions*, St. Augustine contrasts physical light with the divine light. The physical light that draws our eyes to beautiful forms brings delight, but it also poses a certain danger. While he acknowledges that objects of physical beauty are made by God and are good, Augustine expresses concern that they might captivate our hearts and draw us away from the Creator. "But [*God*] is my good, not these," he insists.[1] Augustine then draws upon biblical examples (Tobit, Isaac, Jacob) to suggest that the divine light guides God's people even when their physical eyesight has failed. His conclusion is striking: "This light itself is one, and all those are one who see it and love it."[2] The unity shared among these biblical characters is available to all who are drawn to the light of God. Lesser goods pale in comparison, for the source of their very appeal is their participation in the eternal good of God. Thus, to behold the divine light, the supreme good, is to love it and be moved toward it. To bask in that radiance is to be brought into communion with all who share in it—"all those are one who see it and love it."

In this chapter, we take up the doctrine of the church from the angle of shared participation in the divine light. Not only does our movement toward God draw us together, as Augustine recognized, but so also does

1. Augustine, *Confessions*, X.xxxiv (51) (p. 209 in the Chadwick translation).
2. Augustine, *Confessions*, X.xxxiv (52) (p. 209 in the Chadwick translation).

that movement typically begin with the influence of other people. As we saw in chapter 4, it is often the case that some sort of connection with the community of faith opens a person to a glimpse of the divine radiance. It is doubtless the case that the church's capacity in this regard depends upon—in fact, is nothing other than—the work of the Holy Spirit. And it is also the case that the Spirit can and does move directly upon hearts and minds, as well as through any number of means beyond the church. But the witness of the New Testament is clear that the normative movement of the Holy Spirit flows through the church and draws believers together into the community of faith.

Our reflections on the doctrine of the church, or ecclesiology, will follow the threefold pattern we have used throughout the book. The first section, allure, will take up the proclamation of the gospel as an enduring and essential task of the church across the ages. By framing evangelism in terms of witnessing to the divine light, the community of faith avoids the temptation to center itself in its proclamation. The second progression, movement, will explore the church's work of initiation and formation. For those who respond to the invitation of the gospel, how are they incorporated into the community of faith? And in what ways does the Holy Spirit move in and through the church to form disciples as a people walking in the light? Our final section on joy will focus on the worship life of the church. If the movement of the community of disciples is toward an ever-greater communion with the radiant God, then the church's practices of worship will reflect both proclamation of and delight in the divine light.

Allure: Bearing Witness to the Heavenly Light

We have already seen the repeated use of the phrase "the light of the world" in the Gospel of John. In that Gospel, Jesus uses the phrase to refer to himself (8:12; 9:5; 11:9). But when we turn to the Gospel of Matthew, we find an interesting development. In his Sermon on the Mount, we read the following: "You are the light of the world. A city built on a hill cannot be hid. No one after lighting a lamp puts it under the bushel basket, but on the lampstand, and it gives light to all in the house. In the same way, let your light shine before others, so that they may see your good works and give glory to your Father in heaven" (Matt 5:14–16). Jesus's use of the same phrase to refer to his followers is instructive. Even if we are initially taken aback by the shift in subject from one Gospel to the other, the intertextual echo indicates an essential connection between Christ and his church. The light that Jesus is can be radiated by his disciples to the degree that they attend to him and his teaching. The latter part of this passage suggests that visible obedience to his instruction in the form of good works manifests his light to the world. Just as Jesus visibly reflected the glory that he shares with the Father in his incarnation, now also will the church glorify the Father through works that reflect Christ's teaching.

This connection between the light of Jesus and the church's reflection of that light raises a question. Why should God choose such a vessel, a community of fallible humans, to witness to the divine glory through time and space? Pope Benedict XVI takes this question up with specific reference to the resurrection appearances of Jesus, which are concentrated on the disciples rather than Jesus's opponents. Benedict sees in this an echo of God's pattern of divine revelation, focused as it is on the particular people of Israel. "It is part of the mystery of God that he acts so gently, that he only gradually builds up *his* history within the great history of mankind; that he becomes man and so can be overlooked by his contemporaries and by the decisive forces within history; . . . that he continues to knock gently at the doors of our hearts and slowly opens our eyes if we open our doors to him."[3] This pattern of invitation rather than compulsion, he continues, is a mark of the freedom that makes genuine love for God and others possible. "And yet—is not this the truly divine way? Not to overwhelm with external power, but to give freedom, to offer and elicit love."[4] Yet this divine movement toward the world, offering love and inviting love in return, can only captivate our attention if it reflects truth. When we perceive God's overtures toward us as revealing one who is both beautiful and true, we are drawn in. And it is at this point that Benedict takes up the image of light to indicate the allure of Christ, which is conveyed in the church's witness: "Does not a ray of light issue from Jesus, growing brighter across the centuries, that could not come from any mere man and through which the light of God truly shines into the world? Could the apostolic preaching have found faith and built up a worldwide community unless the power of truth had been at work within it?"[5] Thus the light that shines in and through the church's proclamation only has an enduring effect insofar as its source is God. Earthly cities have their temporary appeal, but the illumined city on the hill is different. The

3. Pope Benedict XVI, *Jesus of Nazareth,* 2:276 (original emphasis).

4. Pope Benedict XVI, *Jesus of Nazareth,* 2:276.

5. Pope Benedict XVI, *Jesus of Nazareth,* 2:276–77.

church's sustained vitality through the centuries depends on its faithfulness in radiating the light of the God who fulfills all desire.

The evangelistic work of the church can thus be envisioned as radiating Christ's light to a darkened world. We see this image taken up in a sermon on the transfiguration by Pantoleon, who compares the light of the gospel to the brightness of dawn:

> The very first sign of dawn's light drives sleep from our eyelids, and when the first grey daylight breaks forth, it scatters the shadows of our dreams. . . . In the same way, as the light of the Gospel floods the house of the universal Church, let the mist of sluggishness fade like night, and let every vain activity, like a tent pitched in dreamland, be folded up; let the inspired songs of our teachers resound from the highest branches of the pulpit, bearing their own witness to the presence of the heavenly light.[6]

Just as the light of dawn breaks the darkness of the night, so also does the divine radiance dispel the shadows of a disordered creation. And yet it is significant that Pantoleon first sees this light flooding the house of the church, to awaken it from sluggishness and vanity. Once illumined in God's radiance, the church can bear witness to the light of heaven. In that respect, the divine light both invigorates the church's evangelistic work and provides the object to which that witness points. Awakened by the light, the community of faith testifies to the God who is light.

These considerations now put us in a position to comprehend the import of Jesus's phrase "children of the light" in the Gospel of John. After hearing Jesus allude to his death on the cross in terms of being "lifted up" in John 12, the crowd responds that they have learned from the law that the Messiah remains forever (v. 34). They are puzzled, therefore, by Jesus's comment about being lifted up. Jesus responds, "the light is with you for a little longer. Walk while you have the light, so that the darkness may not overtake you. If you walk in the darkness, you do not know where you are going. While you have the light, believe in the light, so that you may become children of the light" (vv. 35–36). The time of Jesus's earthly ministry is drawing to a close, as the phrasing of these verses hints. And yet those who believe in the light and walk in the light will not be overtaken by darkness

6. Pantoleon, Deacon and Chartophylax, "Sermon on the Most Glorious Transfiguration of Our Lord and God, Jesus Christ," in Daley, *Light on the Mountain*, 107. Daley suggests that little is known for certain of the time and setting of this sermon, but that there is some good evidence to connect it to a sixth-century Byzantine figure. See Daley, *Light on the Mountain*, 105.

in the season to come. Rather, as children of the light, they will continue to bask in and radiate the divine brilliance to a darkened world. This task will require a great deal of courage, as Jesus's predictions of opposition from the world make clear.

Drawing on the thought of Athanasius, Jaroslav Pelikan suggests that the faith and courage necessary to the church's witness flowed from Christ's radiance. "In the light of the resurrection of Christ," Pelikan writes, the children of the light "could see the light of their own lives, because the illumination that was salvation meant the end of the reign of darkness. Those who had dwelt in the shadow of death had discovered the light of new life in Christ, whose light and warmth were reflected in their faith and courage."[7] What they received from Christ enabled them to fulfill their evangelistic calling to offer hope to a world in need. Again highlighting the work of Athanasius, Pelikan suggests that this involved not only proclamation but also the demonstration of divine power in the very life of the church. This requires an intimate connection between the church and its Lord: "The children of the light were the children of that light which had shone forth in Christ the radiance to grant the illumination of salvation to a darkling world." Pelikan continues, "The new life was the life of light, not merely as moral virtue, but as a participation in the power of God the light. . . . To be children of the light and to shine as lamps meant to be the channels through which the power of being delivered and sustained [reached] the world."[8] This divine power is demonstrated in the new life of the community, reflecting the deliverance from the darkness of sin and prompting a desire to extend the reach of the light.

In both word and deed, then, the community of faith proclaims the good news of salvation to the world. As we have seen, it is not possible to be faithful to this task without abiding in Christ, who is the very ground of that salvation. To this we must add another necessary element: intentionality. While there is doubtless a sense in which immersion in the divine light carries a natural attractiveness to some who have tired of the patterns of the world, the community of disciples has been commissioned to go and make disciples of all nations. Jesus's exhortation to his followers in Matthew 5 to let their light shine before others is now thickened in the post-resurrection commission to his disciples in Matthew 28. This commission from its Lord means that the church is always called to be proactive in witness and

7. Pelikan, *Light of the World*, 107.
8. Pelikan, *Light of the World*, 108–9.

proclamation of the gospel. In this respect, the community of faith can be regarded as a living invitation to the light. And the appeal of that invitation will depend on the degree to which the disciples of Jesus reflect his radiance in their lives and works.

There is one further text in the Gospel of Matthew that illuminates the church's evangelistic imperative. Throughout that gospel, Matthew's tendency to read Old Testament texts christologically is abundantly clear, and the fourth chapter is no exception. In narrating the beginning of Jesus's ministry, Matthew recalls a text of prophetic hope from Isaiah. That text reads: "The people who walked in darkness have seen a great light; those who lived in a land of deep darkness—on them, light has shined" (Isa 9:2). Matthew places the inauguration of Jesus's ministry in the same geographical location, the land of Zebulun and Naphtali, seeing him as the fulfillment of the prophecy of a light to the nations: "'the people who sat in darkness have seen a great light, and for those who sat in the region and shadow of death light has dawned.' From that time Jesus began to proclaim, 'Repent, for the kingdom of heaven has come near'" (Matt 4:16–17). The call to repentance and preparation for the coming kingdom is framed in terms of the emergence of light into a land of darkness and shadow. And the dominical commands to the disciples to shine their light and make disciples of all nations means that the invitation will continue to go out. There is, further, a minor difference between the Isaiah text and the Matthew text that may prompt—for the reader, at least—a picture of what response to the invitation will look like. While Isaiah had the people *walking* in darkness, Matthew renders them as *sitting* in darkness. Whether this is a result of a textual variation or an intentional decision on Matthew's part, the contrast in the canonical form is nonetheless intriguing. Matthew's version conveys darkness as a condition of languishing. Instead of walking, they are not moving at all. Lacking vitality, those without light sit in a region in which death looms. But to see the great light, now focused christologically in Matthew, calls forth movement toward that light. Thus the followers of Jesus, the children of the light, will be a people on the move.

Movement: Joining the Saints in the Light

For those who had been sitting in darkness, seeing the great light dawn in the ministry of Jesus inspires action. At one level, this movement can be understood with reference to the evangelistic mission of the church that we have been exploring—perhaps most clearly exemplified in the great commission of Jesus. Between perceiving the light and shining the light to others, though, there is a necessary step: *becoming* children of the light. So at another level, seeing the radiance of Jesus calls forth initiation into the community of his disciples and formation in the new life that he brings. The people who had previously been sitting in darkness do not walk on their own, but they walk together with those who have perceived the radiance of God in Christ by the Holy Spirit. This entails a natural progression: repentance, conversion, catechesis, and baptism. Such practices of initiation mark one's entrance into the community of faith, beginning a process of formation that will prepare one to share in the divine radiance. While chapter 4 traced the progression of a believer's movement through the stages of disorientation, awareness, and walking in the light, we focus here on the communal context in which that movement is shaped.

A natural place to begin our reflections is Colossians 1, given that text's interest in both initiation and formation. There, the movement from darkness to light is conceived as a divine rescue that results in membership in a new kingdom. Strikingly, this rescue is identified as an act of the first person of the Trinity, emphasizing the Son's work of redemption as fulfilling the direct will of the Father. The saints at Colossae are reminded of the importance of "giving thanks to the Father, who has enabled you to share in the inheritance of the saints in the light. He has rescued us from the power of darkness and transferred us into the kingdom of his beloved Son, in whom we have redemption, the forgiveness of sins" (Col 1:12–14). The forgiveness of sin that comes through the Son entails a transfer of kingdoms. And the community that one now joins as a result is that of the "saints in the light." The church's markers of initiation trace the believer's movement into the kingdom of the Son.

The salient point to notice about the process of Christian initiation is that it involves the entire person. As one moves into the community of the saints in the light, one's will, mind, and body are engaged. We focus here on three practices of initiation: repentance and conversion, catechesis, and baptism. Together these can be conceived as a holistic movement toward the divine light: conversion as a movement of the will, catechesis as the movement of the mind, and baptism as the movement of the body. We will take repentance and conversion together as a single practice of initiation, even though we could mark different shades of meaning between these terms. Repentance signals a turn away from a pattern of sin, and it is attended by a sense of contrition for one's failures. Conversion emphasizes the turn itself, and its frame of reference is simultaneously the new path of light and the old path of darkness (whereas repentance is primarily oriented to the movement away from the old path). Furthermore, it is natural to think of the person repenting as the agent of repentance, while the Holy Spirit is most properly regarded as the agent of conversion. For all of these distinctions, though, we can consider the shift in commitment from self-will to the will of God as one movement of initiation into the church. This shift involves both divine and human agency, with the free response of the latter dependent upon the enabling grace of the former. While conversion is an essentially personal transition, the alignment of one's will with God's both requires communal support and orders one toward a shared life in the Spirit. As Colossians 1:12 suggests, the outcome of the transfer of kingdoms is to give one a share in the inheritance of the saints in the light. In this regard, conversion is best thought of as a communal practice of initiation.

Another essentially communal act of Christian initiation is catechesis. A transformation of the mind is inevitably involved in the movement from darkness to light, and basic instruction in the faith plays an important role in that process. Particularly when dealing with the image of light, however, there is some complexity in sorting through the respective roles of knowledge as a direct gift of God and knowledge that is mediated through the church over time and space. Both elements are present in the Pauline corpus. Ephesians 1 and Colossians 1—texts that we explored in chapter 5 and above, respectively—include prayers for spiritual wisdom and revelation as a gift from God. Indeed, this sense of immediate perception is often what the notion of the divine light calls to mind. Jonathan Edwards's sermon "A Divine and Supernatural Light" works with this understanding of divine light as "immediately imparted to the soul by God, of a different nature from any that is obtained by natural means."[9] Initially, then, it is difficult to imagine what role catechetical instruction might play in the movement of the mind.

Yet there is another stream in the Pauline epistles, one that emphasizes the necessary place of solid teaching. This comes through particularly clearly in the Pastoral epistles, such as in the appeals of 1 Timothy 1:3-7, 1 Timothy 4:6-16, 2 Timothy 4:1-5, and Titus 2:1. These passages highlight the dangers of false teaching and the importance of holding firm to sound

9. Edwards, "A Divine and Supernatural Light," §2 (p. 123 in the Kimnach, Minkema, and Sweeney volume).

doctrine. In a similar way, Paul recalls his own proclamation of the gospel to the believers at Corinth. This reminder in 1 Corinthians 15:1 is followed by a substantial summary of the content of that proclamation: a series of statements, creedal in form, recounting Jesus's death, resurrection, and appearances to the disciples (15:3–8). Paul reminds the Corinthians that he handed these claims on to them "as of first importance," as he had received them. The ongoing catechetical function of this proto-creed is made clear in verses 1–2: these believers stand in this gospel and are being saved through it if they "hold firmly to the message" that Paul proclaimed to them. In that regard, the content of the evangelistic word that was initially proclaimed is reinforced and developed through ongoing teaching of sound doctrine.

The Pauline emphasis on teaching in the churches makes it clear that spiritual understanding given directly by God—of the sort identified in Ephesians and Colossians—does not negate the role of catechesis. On the contrary, it confirms the content of that teaching. In this regard, Edwards provides insight into the relationship between that which is mediated and that which is immediate. He insists that the spiritual light "is not the suggesting of any new truths, or propositions not contained in the word of God." Rather, this light "only gives a due apprehension of those things that are taught in the Word of God."[10] We can detect here an echo of the notion of the illumination of the Holy Spirit that we encountered in chapter 5. For Edwards, then, the proclamation and teaching of Scripture mediates the *content* of our knowledge of God and salvation. And the supernatural light given immediately given by God enables the believer to *perceive the truth* of that knowledge. I have argued elsewhere that we see a similar epistemological move in John Wesley.[11] Wesley appeals to divine testimony, given in Scripture and mediated through the church, to account for the content of our knowledge about God. He then argues that the direct perception of the divine provides the clearest and most reliable evidence of the truth of those beliefs. Both Edwards and Wesley, therefore, understand the direct work of God to enable us to recognize the claims of the faith as true. But the reception of those claims themselves comes through the community of faith passing on what it received through divine revelation. In that respect, there is clearly a necessary role for catechetical instruction in the transformation of the mind that marks one's movement toward the divine light. Both the

10. Edwards, "A Divine and Supernatural Light," I.3, in Kimnach, Minkema, and Sweeney, *The Sermons of Jonathan Edwards*, 125–26.

11. Koskela, "John Wesley," 459–70.

initial teaching of the basics of the faith and continual reminders of that sound teaching are thus part of the church's work of initiation.

Along with the movement of the will and the mind, the transfer into the kingdom of the Son also involves the body. The primary mark of this movement is baptism. It is true that, at a technical level, the sacraments of baptism, confirmation, and the Eucharist are all regarded as sacraments of initiation.[12] But we focus here on baptism for two main reasons. First, there is a sense in which the other two sacraments of initiation depend logically upon baptism. The Catechism of the Catholic Church, drawing from Pope Paul VI's apostolic constitution *Divinae consortium naturae*, likens the sacraments of initiation to the development of a natural life. "The faithful are born anew by Baptism, strengthened by the sacrament of Confirmation, and receive in the Eucharist the food of eternal life."[13] While the new life is strengthened and nourished by the latter two, it is baptism that marks the emergence of new life itself. It is the sacramental point of entry into the community of faith.

Second, the imagery of baptism as a participation in the death and resurrection of Christ signals the movement of the body from the powers of darkness to new life in the kingdom. Of the five aspects of the meaning of baptism outlined in Faith and Order's *Baptism, Eucharist, and Ministry*, this is the first. "Baptism means participating in the life, death, and resurrection of Jesus Christ," that document reads. "Those baptized are no longer slaves to sin, but free. Fully identified with the death of Christ, they are buried with him and are raised here and now to a new life in the power of the resurrection of Jesus Christ, confident that they will also ultimately be one with him in a resurrection like his."[14] The document is drawing here on a recurring Pauline theme. In Romans 6, for example, we see Paul identifying baptism into Christ's death and resurrection as a marker of leaving sin behind and moving into new life in Christ. So verse 4: "Therefore we have been buried with him by baptism into death, so that, just as Christ was raised from the dead by the glory of the Father, so we too might walk in newness of life." Thus baptism is a sign of the transition from sitting in darkness to walking in new life—a life reflecting the Father's glory that was manifested in the resurrection of Jesus.

12. An important historical treatment of the liturgical practices of initiation is offered in Johnson, *The Rites of Christian Initiation*.

13. *Catechism of the Catholic Church*, 1212.

14. *Baptism, Eucharist, and Ministry*, II.A.3.

It should be noted here that our use of the term "body" should not be taken to signal a reductive materialism in terms of the subject of baptism. Rather, we are recognizing that a tangible physical act reflects the initiation of the whole person. In the sense that all sacraments testify to God's saving work in both the material and the spiritual realms, baptism is an act of the body that proclaims the incorporation of the whole person into new life in Christ and thus into Christ's body, the church. This use of the term body can be recognized in Scripture, and we might turn again to a text in Romans for an exemplary case. At the beginning of Romans 12, Paul writes: "I appeal to you therefore, brothers and sisters, by the mercies of God, to present your bodies as a living sacrifice, holy and acceptable to God, which is your spiritual worship. Do not be conformed to this world, but be transformed by the renewing of your minds, so that you may discern what is the will of God—what is good and acceptable and perfect" (v. 1–2). The exhortation to present our bodies as a living sacrifice to God is a way of speaking about presenting the whole person to God. It is not surprising, then, that Paul identifies the transformation of the mind as a corresponding movement to such a living sacrifice. The result is an evident distinction from the patterns of the world, or the darkness one has left behind, as well as the discernment to know good from evil. Offering one's body to share in Christ's death and resurrection in baptism, therefore, is an offering of one's whole being to participate in the new life made possible by the triune God.

Practices of initiation such as these mark the entrance of the believer into the life of the church. But by no means do they bring the process of moving toward the light to an end. On the contrary, they really signal the beginning of a process of formation. This transformative work is empowered by the Holy Spirit in the context of the community of faith. The ongoing instruction, accountability, mutual encouragement—and perhaps most of all, the prayers—of fellow believers are all key means through which one experiences the Spirit's sanctifying work. Here we can return to the Colossians 1 text that we explored above. Immediately preceding the exhortation to give thanks to the Father for bringing the saints from darkness to light is a powerful prayer for their continued formation:

> For this reason, since the day we heard it, we have not ceased praying for you and asking that you may be filled with the knowledge of God's will in all spiritual wisdom and understanding, so that you may lead lives worthy of the Lord, fully pleasing to him, as you bear fruit in every good work and as you grow in the knowledge

of God. May you be made strong with all the strength that comes from his glorious power, and may you be prepared to endure everything with patience.
(Col 1:9–11)

The emphasis on spiritual wisdom and understanding of God's will reinforces the connection of mind and life that we saw above. Knowing God's will enables the kind of life and works to which believers are called. Further, God's power strengthens the community to continue faithfully and patiently in challenging times. Formation for the long haul, then, will be a matter of the Spirit shaping one's entire being—mind, body, and will.

The connection between formation in the community of faith and the theme of light is drawn in striking ways in 2 Peter 1. The text begins with a reminder that God has given everything needed for life and godliness, enabling God's people to escape the world's corruption and become participants in the divine nature (vv. 3–4). This promise draws believers into a chain of increasing maturity, adding to faith the marks of goodness, knowledge, self-control, endurance, godliness, mutual affection, and love (vv. 5–7). Those who neglect such development show themselves to be forgetful of the cleansing of sins of the past (v. 9). Thus, the passage emphasizes the importance of constant reminders of this pattern of formation (v. 12–15). At this point, we encounter a fascinating development in the text. Claiming Petrine authority, the passage recalls the basis of the teaching that grounds the church's practice of formation: the apostles' status as eyewitnesses of the majesty of Jesus. And the specific instance recalled is the revelation of the divine light and glory in the transfiguration of Jesus: "For he received honor and glory from God the Father when that voice was conveyed to him by the majestic glory, saying, 'This is my Son, my Beloved, with whom I am well pleased.' We ourselves heard this voice come from heaven, while we were with him on the holy mountain" (v. 17–18). It would be hard to find a more direct appeal to the perception of the divine light in Jesus as the basis for the church's work of formation. In this case, the particular pattern of maturing faith that is outlined in verses 5–7 is the fruit of the apostles' trustworthy teaching. Believers can trust that this pattern is a sound response to seeing the divine light, the passage contends, because it is passed on by those who saw the transfiguration with their own eyes.

The conclusion of 2 Peter 1 carries the theme of light from the vision of the transfiguration of Jesus to the community of faith. The text turns to the prophetic message conveyed through the apostolic community. The continuity of this community under the teaching of those who witnessed the majesty of Jesus means that readers can be sure that the prophetic message has a divine rather than a human origin (v. 19–21). Concentration on this Spirit-given word will focus the community on the divine light, with the effect that the radiance will emerge in the community like morning light: "You will do well to be attentive to this as to a lamp shining in a dark place, until the day dawns and the morning star rises in your hearts" (v. 19). The movement of ecclesial formation, then, will draw the community toward that divine radiance like a people awaiting the end of a long night. The emergence of the dawn will yield the joy of those who have not only been rescued from darkness but also now bask in the glory that the apostles glimpsed on the mountain.

Joy: Their Faces Reflected the Light

There is a phrase in Psalm 34 that captures concisely the effect of directing attention to God: "Look to him, and be radiant" (34:5). This is a fitting account of what happens in worship, as God's people gaze upon the God who is light. In fact, the context is set earlier in the same psalm in the form of a call to corporate worship: "O magnify the LORD with me, and let us exalt his name together" (v. 3). The practice of worship positions the community of faith to reflect the divine light and to experience the bliss of realizing the purpose for which human beings were created. Yet a question emerges when we consider the connection between movement and formation on the one hand and worship and joy on the other. Throughout this book, we have been considering joy as the culmination of the process of transformation or grace-enabled movement. Yet the practice of worship is certainly not reserved for the end of the journey of sanctification. On the contrary, it marks and even fosters the entire process of transformation. We might ask, therefore: should we think of our second and third progressions as simultaneous or sequential? Does movement lead to joy, or does joy attend the process of movement all along?

The answer is undoubtedly both, but precisely how that is the case is a matter that requires some consideration. The Christian tradition has long recognized a connection between holiness and happiness, as reflected in figures such as Augustine to Thomas Aquinas to John Wesley.[15] Happiness

15. Pinckaers traces this connection with particular clarity as it relates to the Beatitudes in *The Pursuit of Happiness*, especially pp. 23–37.

in this respect is not to be regarded as a feeling of temporary amusement, but rather the condition of fulfilling one's highest end—akin to how we have been treating the category of joy in our discussion. Complete and un-alloyed happiness are possible only in the next life, since only then will our desire for the good be perfectly satiated.[16] But it is also the case that a mea-sure of joy is attainable in this life, to the degree that our lives are ordered in the present to God as our final end. And as Thomas Aquinas points out, we need the friendship of others to realize the measure of happiness that is attainable in this life. For St. Thomas, this is because the cultivation of virtue requires the sharing of good works with other people.[17] We might take hold of this observation in service of a broader point: sanctification is an essentially ecclesial affair, even as it is an essentially personal affair. Precisely as we are formed in holiness by the Spirit in the community of faith, we take greater and greater hold of the joy that attends the fulfillment of our final end. In its worship, the church both acknowledges and delights in the triune God who enables this salvation.

The manner in which worship relates to formation, then, is twofold. At one level, we can understand the liturgical practices of the church as part of the process of formation. In these practices the church embodies the pat-tern of formation outlined in the 2 Peter 1 text explored above, from faith and goodness to mutual affection and love. At another level, the worship life of the church provides a taste of the joy that lies ahead. The Orthodox tradition has long understood the Divine Liturgy, for example, as an en-trance into the joy of heaven. We see a vivid example of this in Alexander Schmemann's account of the Eucharist in *For the Life of the World*: "The Eucharist is the entrance of the Church into the joy of its Lord. And to enter into that joy, so as to be a witness to it in the world, is indeed the very calling of the Church, its essential *leitourgia*, the sacrament by which it 'becomes what it is.'"[18] Schmemann here makes explicit the necessity of this joy in order to fulfill the church's evangelistic mission. He sees the liturgy as the means by which the church can serve as a witness to the world of joy; indeed, this has been so from its earliest period:

16. So Aquinas, *Summa Theologica*, I–II.5.3.

17. Aquinas, *Summa Theologica*, I–II.4.8. St. Thomas takes a rather utilitarian view of other people here, seeing them as necessary for the operation of good—to do good works to them, to delight in their good works, and to be helped by them in doing good works. Even if we should want to say more than this of the role of community in the cultivation of holiness and happiness, we should not say less.

18. Schmemann, *For the Life of the World*, 26.

The early Christians realized that in order to become the temple of the Holy Spirit they must *ascend to heaven* where Christ has ascended. They realized also that this ascension was the very condition of their mission in the world, of their ministry to the world. For there—in heaven—they were immersed in the new life of the Kingdom; and when, after this "liturgy of ascension," they returned to the world, their faces reflected the light, the "joy and peace" of that Kingdom and they were truly its witnesses.[19]

Here we recognize that the allure-movement-joy pattern is not entirely sequential, even if we have detected a logical ordering of these progressions throughout our discussion. While complete joy awaits us in the next life, we get a taste of it in worship, and that taste nourishes both our movement and our witness. Indeed, Schmemann implies that the power of that witness is in the divine light reflecting off of the faces of those who have ascended to heaven in worship.

The idea that worship is a taste of heaven is also evident in the Methodist tradition. It is telling that Lester Ruth's study of early Methodist worship at quarterly meetings is titled *A Little Heaven Below.*[20] The early Methodists' sense that they were experiencing a measure of heaven in this life as they worshiped echoed an image that occasionally emerged in Charles Wesley's published verse. In perhaps the best-known reference, "O For a Thousand Tongues to Sing," it is in response to the divine love that forgives sin that believers can "anticipate [their] heaven below."[21] While this hymn connects the foretaste of eternity explicitly to the reception of and response to God's love, the hymn's title frames worship as the immediate embodiment of that response. The connection is drawn more directly with the practice of communion in another Charles Wesley hymn, "Come, Sinners, to the Gospel Feast." This Eucharistic feast is a means of "knowing *now* your sins forgiven" and "tasting *here* the joys of heaven."[22] A hymn where the link between worship and heaven is developed in particular detail is Charles Wesley's "Come, Let Us Join Our Friends Above." In calling the church to worship, that hymn envisions the saints on earth joining with the saints in heaven:

19. Schmemann, *For the Life of the World,* 28 (original emphasis).

20. Ruth, *A Little Heaven Below.*

21. Charles Wesley, "O For a Thousand Tongues to Sing," in John Wesley, *Collection of Hymns (1780),* 8.

22. *Hymns for Those That Seek,* 64.

Come let us join our friends above
 That have obtain'd the prize,
And on the eagle-wings of love
 To joy celestial rise;
Let all the saints terrestrial sing
 With those to glory gone:
For all the servants of our king
 In earth and heaven are one.[23]

By entering into the worship of God with the departed fellow servants, the church on earth is enabled to rise to joy celestial. As with Schmemann, Wesley recognizes the call of the church to enter into the joy of the Lord.

In worship, both in this life and the next, we see the aim of movement toward the divine light. The people who sat in darkness have seen a great light, and in moving toward that light, they look to God and become radiant. In the midst of their singing, prayer, reading of Scripture, passing of the peace, and most of all in the Eucharist, they receive a taste of the heavenly joy that awaits. It is notable that Pope St. John Paul II identified Jesus's institution of the Eucharist as one of the "mysteries of light," each of which is "a revelation of the Kingdom now present in the very person of Jesus."[24] The church is invited to experience the joy of the kingdom of God in their sojourn through time. But as St. Thomas reminds us, the fullness of that joy lies ahead. What is tasted now is given without measure in the life to come. And worship is not only a way of mediating that joy to us now; the saints "to glory gone" continue to sing in the presence of the God who is light. Thus the joy of worship is the present and the future of Christ's church. In the church's doxology, God's people are given a glimpse of the divine glory. In our final chapter, we turn to their immersion in that glory as we consider the doctrine of Christian hope.

23. Charles Wesley, "Come, Let Us Join Our Friends Above," in John Wesley, *Pocket Hymn Book (1785)*, 19.

24. Pope St. John Paul II, *Rosarium Virginis Mariae*, 21.

7

Christian Hope

"But the Lord Will Be Your Everlasting Light"

THROUGHOUT OUR DISCUSSION OF the divine radiance, the biblical narrative of the transfiguration of Jesus has served as an important signpost. Not only does it offer a revealing glimpse of Christ's divine glory, but it also points to the future that awaits his disciples. The three apostles who set eyes on the brilliance of Jesus on the mountain would someday come to share in the light that they beheld. And those who follow on the basis of their testimony take hold of the same hope. This is a recurring theme in the Christian tradition, and Pseudo-Macarius offers a compelling example:

> For as the body of the Lord was glorified when he climbed the mount and was transfigured into the divine glory and into infinite light, so also the bodies of the saints are glorified and shine like lightning. . . . Similarly, as many lamps are lighted from the one, same fire, so also it is necessary that the bodies of the saints, which are members of Christ, become the same which Christ himself is.[1]

Pseudo-Macarius points here to a hope that is located ecclesiologically precisely because it is grounded christologically. As members of the body of Christ, the saints will be transformed to share in the glory that Christ is. To come fully to terms with what is accomplished in Christ and mediated by the Spirit through the church, we must therefore attend to eschatology.

It is not only the personal hope of transfiguration that occupies our attention here. Creation itself, which began to take shape with the emergence of light at the divine command, also has a share in the freedom of the glory

---

1. Pseudo-Macarius, *Homilies*, 15.38 (pp. 122–23 in the Maloney translation).

to be revealed (Rom 8:19–25). David Bentley Hart sees a sign of this hope in the icon of the transfiguration:

> The icon also, however, offers us a glimpse of the eschatological horizon of salvation; for the same light that the three disciples were permitted to see break forth from the body of Christ will, in the fullness of time, enter into and transform all of creation, with that glory that the Son had with the Father before the world began (John 17:5), and that the whole of creation awaits with groans of longing and travail (Rom. 8:19–23).[2]

The created light of Genesis 1:3–5, as St. Ambrose suggested, was a means for creaturely eyes to take in some semblance of the invisible divine light. Good and beautiful though it is, such physical light is not divine and thus is not capable of transforming creation. By contrast, Hart suggests that the divine light that shone through the transfigured body of Christ is so capable. As with human beings, the hope of creation itself is that very light infusing it and drawing it into the divine glory—without ever losing the distinction between Creator and creation.

As the Romans 8 text reminds us, of course, creation still groans and the full revelation of the divine glory remains in the future. The full manifestation of God's redemptive work is something that the community of faith yet awaits. The church's eschatology, its doctrine of Christian hope, emerges as a response to the gap between things as they are and things as they shall be. The people who sat in darkness have seen a great light, but they continue to walk because they have not yet been fully immersed into that light. But why should they suppose their journey will reach its intended conclusion? What is the basis of the church's hope? The formal category we must attend to here is divine promise. Both the content and the assurance of Christian hope emerges from the revelation of God's intention to bring the work of salvation to its full consummation. That promise is mediated through a combination of revelatory divine action—most centrally the resurrection of Jesus—and the Spirit-guided reception of divine revelation in the community of faith. And sacred Scripture stands at the heart of the Holy Spirit's movement in the community of faith to receive the self-disclosure of God. The biblical texts witness to the revelatory action of God, and the Spirit works within the church to guide its prayerful interpretation of the word of God. This process yields the object of Christian hope, which is God's reconciliation of all things, as well as the various aspects that mark

---

2. David Bentley Hart, "Foreword," in Nes, *The Uncreated Light*, xiii–xiv.

that reconciliation. These include the coming of Christ, the resurrection of the dead, the final judgment, and the vision of God.

Our exploration of eschatology will center on the divine radiance, following our standard threefold pattern. The first section on allure will take up the first two markers, the return of Christ and the resurrection of the dead. The church's continual confession of these divine promises offers hope in the midst of the darkness that remains in creation. The second progression, movement, will examine the theme of divine judgment. An eschatological reckoning awaits all creation in the final judgment, and for human beings this represents the final acknowledgment of the Spirit's work that has prepared them for union with God. Finally, our exploration of joy will focus on the vision of God, which represents full immersion into the divine light. After judgment has affirmed the extent of divine grace in the work of sanctification and purification, those in Christ will experience what the disciples could only see on the mountain of transfiguration. They who have seen only in a mirror, dimly, will then see face to face (1 Cor 13:12).

Allure: The Land of Light and Joy

In our first chapter, we encountered the vision in Isaiah 60 of the brilliant glory of God shining over Jerusalem. The promise that the nations would gather to the divine light radiating upon the holy city conveys something of the sheer beauty of God. But still, this vision took the form of a promise for the future. While there is undoubtedly a concrete post-exilic hope expressed in this text, it is natural for Christians to read this vision as a glimpse of the culmination of God's saving work at the end of history. And that promise takes shape in a remarkable form in verses 19–20:

> The sun shall no longer be your light by day, nor for brightness shall the moon give light to you by night; but the LORD will be your everlasting light, and your God will be your glory. Your sun shall no more go down, or your moon withdraw itself; for the LORD will be your everlasting light, and your days of mourning shall be ended.

The created sources of light that must suffice in a condition of darkness, even as they come and go, will give way to the glory of God that shines eternally. The nations are drawn to the allure of the divine radiance, and they need not worry that it will disappear. For the light that is a hope for God's people on their sojourn will be an ever-present reality at its end.

We find an unmistakable New Testament echo of the Isaiah 60 text in the vision of Revelation 21. Descending from heaven in this vision is the new Jerusalem, a city in which God will make his home with mortals (21:3–4). In this new order of things, there will be no death, mourning, crying, or pain. When an angel carries the narrator away in the spirit to a high mountain to get a view of the city, a remarkable observation follows: "I saw no temple in the city, for the temple is the Lord God the Almighty and the Lamb. And the city has no need of sun or moon to shine on it, for the glory of God is its light, and its lamp is the Lamb" (21:22–23). As in the Isaiah text, the divine glory shining throughout the city renders the lesser physical light of the sun and the moon unnecessary. Given this description, one might expect that the brilliance of God's glory would subsume creatures completely, leaving little trace of their particular identities or histories. Yet the verses that follow suggest a rather different picture. The light of the nations' glory is indeed subsumed, but it is brought into the presence of the divine glory as an offering: "The nations will walk by its light, and the kings of the earth will bring their glory into it. Its gates will never be shut by day—and there will be no night there. People will bring into it the glory and the honor of the nations" (21:24–26). As verse 27 makes clear, the glory of the nations that is brought into the city is not identical to earthly glory as it is conceived in history. We are told that nothing unclean will enter the city, and neither will anyone who practices "abomination or falsehood." Thus the pale imitation of true glory that often passes for earthly honor, which is won through evil and deceit, will have no place in the light of the new Jerusalem. But the true glory of the nations is ultimately a reflection of the divine radiance that goes out to creation and is offered back to God in the grace-enabled procession into the heavenly city. It is hard to imagine a better picture of the divine light subsuming without obliterating the particular histories of God's creatures.

These texts capture two crucial theological insights: the radiant beauty of God that draws toward it all who will see it, and the completeness of our immersion in God's light that awaits in the life to come. For now, we still must make our way in the conditions of a darkened creation, relying as we can on such tenuous goods as light from the sun and the moon. But Christians look forward to a day when these goods will give way to the ultimate good and the Lord will be our everlasting light. What, then, lies between here and there? What works of God yet to come mark the fulfillment of the divine promise? We find a first indicator at the end of Revelation, in the penultimate verse of the Bible: "Come, Lord Jesus" (22:20). Indeed, the anticipation of the parousia, the return of Christ, has been an enduring feature of the Christian experience through the generations. The Nicene Creed affirms the belief that "he will come again in glory," reflecting a conviction that appears repeatedly in the New Testament. The public revelation of Jesus's glory in the parousia is awaited eagerly by Christians because it signals the fulfillment of the divine promise to usher them into that glory.

While the expected coming of Christ is a sign of hope, we cannot avoid the foreboding quality of many biblical texts that allude to it. This is true in particular of Jude, as well as many references to the parousia in the Gospels. There is no doubt that this ominous language stems from the connection between the return of Christ and judgment, which we will take up below. But in the midst of such language, there are yet indicators of the light to come. An intriguing example appears in Matthew 24. On the Mount of Olives, Jesus's disciples ask him to reveal signs of his coming and of the end of the age. After warning them of the difficulty that lies ahead, Jesus tells them:

> Immediately after the suffering of those days the sun will be darkened, and the moon will not give its light; the stars will fall from heaven, and the powers of heaven will be shaken. Then the sign of the Son of Man will appear in heaven, and then all the tribes of the earth will mourn, and they will see "the Son of Man coming on the clouds of heaven" with power and great glory.
> (Matt 24:29–30)

Given our exploration of Isaiah 60 and Revelation 21 above, we cannot help but take note of the reference to the darkening of the sun and the extinguishing of the light of the moon. This intertextual echo offers a ray of hope to accompany the threatening cosmic signs in Jesus's discourse. The reference to the end of these physical sources of light, which clears the way for the vision of the glory of the Son of Man, signals the end of the present order of creation. And readers attuned to the passages in Isaiah and Revelation will take these images as a cue for the emergence of the everlasting light of the Lord. The language of the sun and moon going dark points us toward the new creation in which the glory of God shines eternally. Alongside the note of judgment, which is properly to be feared, there is a signal of the fulfillment of the hope of God's people to bask in the everlasting light of the Lord.

The anticipation of the return of Christ is a constant in the Christian life, but it is marked in a particular way during the season of Advent. The liturgical season in which we long for the arrival of Christ's birth at Christmas is simultaneously a season of earnestly awaiting his return. There is an etymological hint of the latter hope in the name of the season, as the Latin *adventus* and the Greek *parousia* share a similar semantic range around the idea of arrival or coming. The orientation of Advent toward the second coming of Jesus is a particular point of emphasis in Fleming Rutledge's *Advent: The Once and Future Coming of Jesus Christ*. This remarkable collection of sermons brings out the interplay of darkness and light during this season, both liturgically and spiritually. "Advent begins in the dark," Rutledge writes,

> and moves toward the light—but the season should not move too quickly or too glibly, lest we fail to acknowledge the depth of the darkness. As our Lord Jesus tells us, unless we see the light of God clearly, what we call light is actually darkness: "how great is that darkness!" (Matt 6:23). Advent bids us take a fearless inventory of the darkness: the darkness without and the darkness within.[3]

Advent is not, therefore, a season in which we find hope by ignoring the darkness of sin and despair. Rather, it is a season of hope because it takes full measure of that darkness, so that we may rightly see the light of Christ as salvation.

Throughout her volume of sermons, Rutledge's reflections on light and darkness are framed by the Collect for the First Sunday of Advent in the *Book of Common Prayer*. In that prayer, the movement from darkness to light is ordered primarily toward the second coming of Jesus, without neglecting the birth of Jesus at Christmas:

> Almighty God, give us the grace that we may cast away the works of darkness, and put upon us the armor of light, now in the time of this mortal life in which thy Son Jesus Christ came to visit us in great humility; that in the last day, when he shall come again in his glorious majesty to judge both the quick and the dead, we may rise to the life immortal; through him who liveth and reigneth with thee and the Holy Ghost, one God, now and for ever. *Amen.*[4]

The light that appeared in the incarnation of Jesus prepares us for the life immortal, which is ushered in by his return in glory. In Advent, the church walks in increasing light as longing gives way to fulfillment. A visual

3. Rutledge, *Advent*, 314–15.
4. *Book of Common Prayer* (1979), 159.

reflection of this can be found in the relatively recent practice of lighting candles on the Advent wreath on Sundays during this season. Each candle intensifies the light as the church moves closer to the birth of Jesus liturgically and the return of Jesus eschatologically.

The first Advent Collect also looks forward to the hope that in the last day "we may rise to the life immortal." And here, in the promise of resurrection, we find a second marker of the fulfillment of Christian hope. "We look for the resurrection of the dead," the Nicene Creed concludes, "and the life of the world to come." We saw above that the second coming of Jesus, the light of the world, signals the passing of darkness and the manifestation of the everlasting light. So also in the resurrection of the dead we find fulfillment of the promise that death will not have the final victory. The promise is given in the resurrection of Christ, with the Spirit's witness in Scripture offering the interpretive key to understand it. We should attend, therefore, to texts that link the fact of Christ's resurrection with the hope of our own. The Pauline witness is important in this regard, and 1 Corinthians 15 is especially noteworthy. Here Paul insists on two fundamental convictions: first, that Christ's resurrection assures the future general resurrection of the dead, and second, that hope in our own resurrection is essential if the Christian message is to be a word of hope. His rhetorical strategy begins in verses 12–14 with a series of counterfactuals: "Now if Christ is proclaimed as raised from the dead, how can some of you say there is no resurrection of the dead? If there is no resurrection of the dead, then Christ has not been raised; and if Christ has not been raised; then our proclamation has been in vain and your faith has been in vain." This leads up to the powerful concluding counterfactual in verse 19: "If for this life only we have hoped in Christ, we are of all people most to be pitied." The truth of Christian preaching and the meaning of the Christian life depend, he contends, on the realization of the promise of everlasting life. And in verse 20, Paul leaves no doubt about the status of this promise: "But in fact Christ has been raised from the dead, the first fruits of those who have died." The affirmation that the Lord is risen is simultaneously an affirmation that the dead shall rise in the last day. Those in Christ await this resurrection as a marker of the light of the life immortal.

In chapter 3, we noted the prevalence of light in Easter liturgies across the various Christian churches. Given the connection between the resurrection of Jesus and our own hope of resurrection, which we have been tracing in 1 Corinthians 15, it is not surprising to find that light is a common theme in funeral rites as well. Rite One for the Burial of the Dead in the

Book of Common Prayer provides a worthy example. That liturgy includes a prayer that God grant the departed "entrance into the land of light and joy, in the fellowship of thy saints."[5] Later in the same service, we find a prayer that links the hope of the resurrection to our end of basking in God's glory: "Grant us, with all who have died in the hope of the resurrection, to have our consummation and bliss in thy eternal and everlasting glory."[6] Near the end of the rite, the prayer of committal alludes to the words of 2 Esdras 2:35: "let light perpetual shine upon" the deceased.[7] The resurrection we await beyond death, secured in the risen Jesus, represents the fulfillment of the hope to walk in the everlasting glory of the Lord.

The allure of the divine light captures the attention of the nations, offering them hope in the midst of darkness. They are drawn to the beauty of the Lord's radiance and sustained by the promise that they shall bask in that light forever. That eternal bliss is the ultimate object of their hope, but between here and there, two concrete markers at the end of history orient the church's eschatological gaze. These divine acts that we confess in expectation, the return of the Lord and the resurrection of the dead, will signal our nearness to the everlasting light. Therefore, they also function as objects of joyful hope. And yet there is another concrete marker that calls forth a more sobering response within us. This divine act is also part of the church's eschatological confession; namely, the final judgment. Together with the parousia and the resurrection, judgment can be seen as a portal to life in the eternal light of God. In this sense, it constitutes the final dimension of our movement toward the divine radiance.

Movement: The Grace of God Had Delivered Them

We have already noted the confession of the return of Jesus in glory and the resurrection of the dead in the Nicene Creed. Between them in the text we find the affirmation of the judgment of the living and the dead. In fact, the language of the Creed indicates a purposive link between the parousia and the judgment: "He will come again with glory to judge the living and the dead." This connection is suggested in Scripture, most directly in 1 Corinthians 4. In that text, Paul minimizes the import of human judgment in light of the coming divine judgment. "It is the Lord who judges me," he

5. *Book of Common Prayer* (1979), 470.
6. *Book of Common Prayer* (1979), 481.
7. *Book of Common Prayer* (1979), 486.

writes. "Therefore do not pronounce judgment before the time, before the Lord comes, who will bring to light the things now hidden in darkness and will disclose the purposes of the heart" (4:4–5). This judgment is no less a marker of hope than the return of Christ and the resurrection, but it takes a bit more work to see how this is the case. For consciousness of impending judgment elicits a measure of unease if not outright fear. Rowan Williams suggests that this is not only psychologically understandable but spiritually appropriate. He writes,

> death is a nakedness to which we must all come, a spiritual strip-ping, as we are confronted by God. The identities we have made, that we have pulled around ourselves like a comfortable dressing-gown or a smart suit will dissolve, and what is deepest in us, what we most want, what we most care about, will be laid bare. We are right to feel apprehensive about that, and we are wrong to brush away the sense of proper fear before God's judgment, however much we dislike the extravagant or hysterical expressions of it that have characterized some ages of Christian history. To the degree to which we don't know ourselves—a pretty high degree for nearly all of us—we are bound to think very soberly indeed of this moment of truth.[8]

Our trepidation in this regard is an indicator of the seriousness of sin and of the extent to which we have caused harm to ourselves and to others. It is far easier to avoid taking stock of the ways we have walked in darkness. The church's confession that Christ will judge us all not only affirms an eschatological truth, but it also fosters spiritual sobriety by prompting us to face the reality of our own actions and dispositions.

Where can we find a word of hope, then, in our acknowledgment that we will be called to account for our lives? The first response must center on Jesus. As the one who has made atonement for sin and stands as our advocate, Christ has made the coming judgment a sign of hope without diminishing its seriousness. We can give thanks that in judgment we stand before the one who showed his love by dying for us while we were yet sin-ners (Rom 5:8). In that light, we are not only judged *by* Christ but also *in* Christ. Williams continues, "The Eastern Orthodox Liturgy asks for 'a good answer before the terrible judgment seat of Christ.' It is worth praying for, in the knowledge that such a 'good answer' can only be provided by the one who has promised to be our advocate, the truth in person."[9] In a similar

8. Williams, *Tokens of Trust*, 146–47.
9. Williams, *Tokens of Trust*, 147.

way, Pope Benedict XVI argues that the cross transforms judgment from a marker of human failure to a sign of divine grace: "But the cross does not reveal only man; it also reveals God. God is such that he identifies himself with man right down into this abyss and that he judges him by saving him. In the abyss of human failure is revealed the still more inexhaustible abyss of divine love."[10] The grace of God that was offered by the Son at Calvary and is received by each believer in the Spirit is affirmed in judgment. This is why Paul can conclude his reflection on Christ's coming judgment on a positive note: "Then each one will receive commendation from God" (1 Cor 4:5).

A word of caution is in order at this point. While the grace of God is doubtless the ground of any hope that we have in the final judgment, our account of grace must be properly nuanced. Our reflections so far, taken on their own, could lead to the impression that grace substitutes for our actual transformation rather than enabling it. Such an impression would undermine the very purpose for which grace was given: to make us the kind of people who can be immersed in the divine light. Therefore, we must include a second response to the question of how the coming judgment can be a word of hope. This second response centers on the work of the Spirit in forming us in the likeness of Christ. Here we recognize that divine judgment does not only include forgiveness of our sins; it also includes the affirmation of what God's grace has accomplished in the form of changed lives. We see in numerous biblical texts, for example, that judgment is oriented toward what one has actually done during one's life. Jesus's teaching about the judgment of the nations in Matthew 25:31–46 focuses on providing food, drink, and clothing for those in need, as well as visiting those who are sick and in prison. In 2 Corinthians 5:10, Paul leaves little doubt about the basis for judgment: "For all of us must appear before the judgment seat of Christ, so that each may receive recompense for what has been done in the body, whether good or evil."

Recognizing that our works are subject to judgment before Christ does not for a moment undermine the necessity or priority of divine grace in enabling our good works. Rather, it shows that grace has a tangible effect in the lives of those it touches. And the judgment of Christ is oriented toward the full scope of the work of grace, not merely the forgiveness of past sins. For those who welcome in the Spirit the grace that is offered through the work of Christ, this judgment can be received as a word of good news. Instead of

10. Pope Benedict XVI (Joseph Cardinal Ratzinger), *Introduction to Christianity*, 293.

anticipating with dread the light of judgment that reveals our failures, we can look forward in hope to the unveiling of good works brought about by the Spirit's gracious work. Jesus highlights this contrast in his conversation with Nicodemus in John 3. Jesus explains that the Son was sent into the world to save rather than to condemn the world (v. 17). Those who welcome this overture of grace by believing in Jesus are not condemned, but those who do not believe are already condemned (v. 18). What follows is a remarkably clear expression of the contrasting attitudes toward judgment, depending on one's orientation to Jesus: "And this is the judgment, that the light has come into the world, and people loved darkness rather than light because their deeds were evil. For all who do evil hate the light and do not come to the light, so that their deeds may not be exposed. But those who do what is true come to the light, so that it may be clearly seen that their deeds have been done in God" (vv. 19–21). Judgment here is essentially a revelation of what has been done, and it is understandable why people would shrink back from it apart from the healing of divine grace. Yet those who have welcomed the coming of grace in Jesus move toward the light of judgment—not so that they may be celebrated, but so that it may be seen that their good works were done in God. It is for the purpose of glorifying God and recognizing the extent of divine grace that the church confesses the judgment of the living and the dead as a word of hope.

Such an account of grace and judgment was developed with particular clarity in the mature thought of John Wesley. Wesley contended that faith is the only immediate and direct necessity for both justification, the forgiveness of one's sins, and sanctification, one's real transformation by the power of God. But he also insisted that both repentance and works that align with repentance are necessary in a remote and conditional sense. That is, if one has time and opportunity to show the fruits of faith in good works—the thief on the cross served as his exception here—then one must do so. These works do not save, but they are the inevitable fruit of the faith by which one is saved.[11] This interaction of divine grace and human response draws people by the Spirit's power toward holiness and happiness.

This is the vision of salvation that Wesley brought to his treatment of the final judgment. His sermon "The Great Assize" offered an extended set of reflections on judgment. Wesley emphasized the universality of the

11. Perhaps the clearest expression of this account can be found in John Wesley's sermon "The Scripture Way of Salvation," I.3–III.13, in Collins and Vickers, *The Sermons of John Wesley*, 584–89.

judgment, which will immediately follow the resurrection of the dead: "Every man, every woman, every infant of days that ever breathed the vital air will then hear the voice of the Son of God, and start into life, and appear before him."[12] The picture of judgment that Wesley drew was detailed and penetrating. Not only will all of the words and actions of each person be brought out into the open, but also the circumstances that accompanied them. This is necessary in God's wisdom, since those circumstances may have "lessened or increased the goodness or badness of" those words and actions. But judgment does not stop there. As was his style, Wesley strung together a series of biblical allusions to suggest an inward dimension as well: "Yea, he 'will bring to light' not 'the hidden works of darkness' only, but the very 'thoughts and intents of the heart.' And what marvel? For he 'searcheth the reins,' and understandeth all our thoughts.' 'All things are naked and open to the eyes of him with whom we have to do.'" The result of this is that the degree of righteousness and unrighteousness in each person will be clearly seen.[13]

Wesley's vivid description of our vulnerability in this moment, however, is set against the background of his confidence in divine grace. The purpose of judgment is neither to humiliate or exalt human beings for their actions, but rather to celebrate the power of God in bringing sinners to holiness. He wrote:

> It is apparently and absolutely necessary, for the full display of the glory of God, for the clear and perfect manifestation of his wisdom, justice, power, and mercy toward the heirs of salvation, that all the circumstances of their life should be placed in open view, together with all their tempers, and all the desires, thoughts, and intents of their hearts. Otherwise how would it appear out of what a depth of sin and misery the grace of God had delivered them?

For those who have received this grace, the revelation of the Spirit's transformative work is followed by their entrance into the joy of the divine light. Wesley used the language of Matthew 13:43 and Psalm 36:8 to convey at least something of their reward:

> And in the discovery of the divine perfections the righteous will rejoice with joy unspeakable; far from feeling any painful sorrow or

12. John Wesley, "The Great Assize," II.4, in Collins and Vickers, *The Sermons of John Wesley*, 640.

13. John Wesley, "The Great Assize," II.5–7, in Collins and Vickers, *The Sermons of John Wesley*, 640.

shame for any of those past transgressions which were long since
blotted out as a cloud, washed away by the blood of the Lamb. . . .
"Then shall the righteous shine forth as the sun in the kingdom
of their Father," and shall "drink of those rivers of pleasure which
are at God's right hand for evermore." But here all description falls
short; all human language fails![14]

In this portrait, the judgment of Christ is the acknowledgment of the entire
work of God in bringing about salvation. Furthermore, it serves as a portal
to full immersion into the divine light.

The allure of the divine light draws the eyes of our hope to the return
of Christ in glory and the new life of the resurrection. Those works of God
are good news insofar as we welcome the Spirit's work of transformation
that leads us out of darkness and into the light. The extent of God's grace in
this movement is revealed at the judgment seat of Christ. Celebrated there
will be not only the forgiveness of sins but the good works and dispositions
that have been enabled by the mercy of God. The culmination of this divine
action is that we are prepared to enter into the joy of light unfiltered. The vision of God that lies beyond judgment is simultaneously union with God.[15]
To see the light is to be infused with the light, as we saw in our opening
reflections on the transfiguration. The joy that has been tasted along the
journey—in the first glimpse of the light, in the experience of God's saving grace, in the worship that draws Christ's church into an experience of
heaven—will then be present in full, when hope gives way to reality.

Joy: We Shall Be Struck by His Blazing Light

"He who beholds the divine light," writes Bishop Kallistos Ware, "is perme-
ated by it through and through, so that his body shines with the glory that
he contemplates."[16] At the end of his sermon "The Great Assize," Wesley
strikes a similar note. He calls upon the vision of Revelation 21–22, where

---

14. John Wesley, "The Great Assize," II.10–III.1, in Collins and Vickers, *The Sermons of John Wesley*, 641–42.

15. It is worth noting that the Catholic Church draws a distinction between an indi-
vidual's particular judgment by Christ at death, after which the soul can enjoy the beatific
vision, and the judgment at the second coming of Jesus and the day of resurrection, when
the soul is reunited with the body to share in the beatific vision. See the *Catechism of the
Catholic Church*, 1021–23 and 1051–52.

16. Ware, *The Orthodox Way*, 127.

God will dwell with his people and "they shall see his face."[17] Wesley suggests that at this point, they "shall have the nearest access to, and thence the highest resemblance of him. This is the strongest expression in the language of Scripture to denote the most perfect happiness."[18] The connection between the vision of God and the perfection of our joy is a final central element of the Christian doctrine of hope. To behold the light of God directly is to be immersed in it, and as daunting as such a thought is, it reflects our deepest longing. To get in touch with that desire, we need to glimpse the light in this life in all of the ways we have been exploring in this book. But those glimpses point us beyond this life, to the eternal realization of that hope. As Julian of Norwich suggests, such pointers can sustain us in seasons of darkness: "And when woe ends, our eyes shall suddenly be opened, and in the brightness of light our sight will be clear, and this light is God our Maker and the Holy Ghost in Christ Jesus our Savior. Thus I saw and understood that our faith is our light in our night, light which is God, our everlasting day."[19]

An important biblical text in shaping the Christian hope of the beatific vision is Exodus 33–34. Moses's encounter with God at Sinai conveys the weight of seeing the divine glory, even as Moses is denied this experience directly. When Moses asks to see the glory of the Lord, he is instructed to stand at a particular place on the rock. The Lord covers Moses until his glory passes by, and then the cover is removed so that Moses can see his back. But Moses is told that no one can see the face of God and live (33:18–23). This sense of reverence is intensified when Moses descends from the mountain with his face shining, prompting fear in those who saw him (34:30). Yet even while acknowledging the awe of this scene, Christian readers throughout the generations have shared Moses's desire to see God. In fact, Arthur Michael Ramsey suggests that this is ultimately the deepest desire of us all: "To the last man's quest remains what it was in the days of Moses—the *seeing* of God. The Christian does not despise as carnal the ancient longing: 'Shew me, I pray thee, thy glory.'"[20]

17. The King James Version is used here, since that is the version that Wesley was quoting.

18. John Wesley, "The Great Assize," III.5, in Collins and Vickers, *The Sermons of John Wesley*, 644.

19. Julian of Norwich, *Revelations of Divine Love*, Long Text 83 (p. 177 in the Spearing translation).

20. Ramsey, *The Glory of God*, 82.

We encounter a striking example of Ramsey's point if we return to the transfiguration homily of Anastasius of Sinai, which we explored in chapter 4. Anastasius reflects at length in that homily on the appearance of Moses on the mountain of Jesus's transfiguration. After crossing from this life to the next, Moses is finally able to see what he longed for. "Moses, then, entered the land of promise as if he were summoned from some exile, the receiver of the law coming up to his Lord on Mount Thabor, bearing the tablets of the law; the servant stood before his master in ecstasy, since he was gazing on divine power in human form."[21] Moses's request to see the divine glory, partially granted on Sinai, is thus granted more fully in the life beyond death. The vision of the three disciples on the mountain of transfiguration, for Anastasius, is a window to the joy Moses now experiences. The depth of longing for God is revealed even more clearly in its fulfillment. We see this in a discourse that Anastasius puts into the mouth of Moses to explain the request of Exodus 33:18:

> "Show me your glory"—let me truly come to know you, reveal yourself to me—"if I have found favor in your sight." For nothing in the world is more delightful to me than to see you, and to be filled with your glory, your beauty, your image, your light, your speech, your revealed presence—when your dwelling has been unveiled before men and women, which once you foreshadowed to me in Mystery.[22]

Throughout Anastasius's reflections, the note of joy is sounded repeatedly in connection with the vision of God. While Moses was granted a glimpse of that glory in this life, the fullness of joy lay ahead in the next.

The convergence of light, joy, and the sight of God is also present in the eschatological vision of Pseudo-Dionysius. Near the beginning of *The Divine Names*, he offers a picture of our end that resonates with the theme of transfiguration. He begins by acknowledging the role of Scripture as the means by which we learn of the divine mysteries.[23] While Scripture gives witness to the divine promises that constitute the church's hope, Pseudo-Dionysius also recognizes a crucial place for "the hidden tradition of our inspired teachers, a tradition at one with Scripture."[24] Initiated into this community of interpretation, we learn what God has in store for us beyond

21. Anastasius of Sinai, "Homily," in Daley, *Light on the Mountain*, 171.
22. Anastasius of Sinai, "Homily," in Daley, *Light on the Mountain*, 173.
23. Pseudo-Dionysius, *The Divine Names*, I.4 (p. 51 in the Luibheid translation).
24. Pseudo-Dionysius, *The Divine Names*, I.4 (p. 52 in the Luibheid translation).

this life. "But in time to come," he writes, "when we are incorruptible and immortal, when we have come at last to the blessed inheritance of being like Christ, then, as Scripture says, 'we shall always be with the Lord' [1 Thess 4:17, KJV]." At the end of the journey toward the likeness of Christ, we are prepared for the vision of God. "In most holy contemplation we shall be ever filled with the sight of God shining gloriously around us as once it shone for the disciples at the divine transfiguration." The sight of God brings forth a mysterious union with God, and Pseudo-Dionysius calls upon the image of light once again to paint the scene: "And there we shall be, our minds away from passion and from earth, and we shall have a conceptual gift of light from him and, somehow, in a way we cannot know, we shall be united with him and, our understanding carried away, blessedly happy, we shall be struck by his blazing light."[25]

The pattern we have traced throughout this book is in many ways summarized in these reflections from Pseudo-Dionysius. We are captivated by the allure of the divine light, shining in creation and most clearly in the incarnate Son. We move toward that light in the power of the Holy Spirit, who shapes us in the likeness of Christ and prepares us to radiate that light in union with God. The Spirit draws us into a traditioned community, walking together in the light, anticipating heaven in its worship. And finally, in the sight of God, we become light—"all light, all face, all eye," in the words of Pseudo-Macarius that we encountered in our Introduction.[26] For those who by grace come to share in that light, there is unending and indescribable joy. The hope of such happiness was expressed, as usual, with particular beauty by Charles Wesley in a hymn to the triune God. His lyric of praise, addressed in this stanza to the Holy Spirit, forms a fitting final word:

> Not angel tongues can tell
> Thy love's extatic height;
> The glorious joy unspeakable,
> The beatific sight![27]

25. Pseudo-Dionysius, *The Divine Names*, I.4 (pp. 52–53 in the Luibheid translation).

26. Pseudo-Macarius, *Homilies*, 1.2 (p. 37 in the Maloney translation).

27. Charles Wesley, "Father, in Whom We Live," in John Wesley, *Pocket Hymn Book* (*1785*), 79. Note: This hymn is now more commonly known as "Maker, in Whom We Live."

Afterword

THE INFLUENCES THAT GIVE rise to any book are a combination of the known and the unknown. Many key voices that have shaped an author's outlook will be fairly clear to the author and readers alike. Others, though, operate at a more subtle level. A text that captured our attention years ago can remain influential in ways that we don't always (at least initially) recognize. Two works in particular have left an imprint on this book, one more obvious and one more subtle.

The influence of the first may be apparent by its use throughout the foregoing discussion. One of the joys of any academic conference is wandering the book exhibit and browsing the offerings. At the annual meeting of the American Academy of Religion and Society of Biblical Literature one year, I happened upon Brian E. Daley's remarkable collection of Greek patristic and Byzantine sermons on the transfiguration. This volume, called *Light on the Mountain*, instantly captivated me. A common ritual on the trip home from AAR/SBL is to begin reading the newly discovered treasures from that year, leaving untouched the papers in need of grading that had been placed in the carry-on with good intentions. The trip home that particular year was spent entirely in the world of these homilies. The deft theological use of light, with all its multivalence, in those sermons prompted a number of the reflections that show up in these pages.

The influence of the second work may be less obvious from what I have written. Indeed, only gradually did I come to realize the imprint of Dante's *Paradiso* on this project. I first read the *Divine Comedy* in high school. But it was as a college undergraduate that I recall being drawn to Dante's use of light imagery. I remember distinctly writing a paper on light in the *Divine Comedy* for a theology class on the theme of journey, meal, and song. While shuffling through a number of boxes above the garage in the late stages of this project could not uncover that essay, the interest that drove it has remained strong across the succeeding decades. Once you begin looking for allusions to the divine radiance in Scripture and the Christian tradition, you begin seeing them all over.

Given my lingering sense of an unpaid debt to Dante, at least in terms of direct references to his poem, I think it appropriate to conclude by turning to the climax of the *Paradiso*. When Dante is finally granted the beatific vision at the end of his journey, light fills the entire scene. As he struggles to find the words for what he is trying to take in, he gives thanks for the grace that enabled the all-consuming sight for which his soul had yearned:

> Oh grace abounding that had made me fit
> to fix my eyes on the eternal light
> until my vision was consumed in it![1]

Just before the three circles of the Trinity emerge in the light that he beholds, Dante expresses the sense that this light sums up all that he could desire. His attention is so fixed on its brilliance that nothing could divert it.

> Experiencing that Radiance, the spirit
> is so indrawn it is impossible
> even to think of ever turning from It.[2]

May each of us be drawn into that radiance to the degree we are granted in this life, and may we be prepared by divine grace to behold it directly in the next.

---

1. Dante, *Paradiso*, XXXIII.82–84 (p. 892 in the Ciardi translation).
2. Dante, *Paradiso*, XXXIII.100–102 (p. 892 in the Ciardi translation).

Bibliography

Alighieri, Dante. *The Divine Comedy: The Inferno, The Purgatorio, and the Paradiso.* Translated by John Ciardi. New York: New American Library, 2003.

Ambrose. *Hexameron, Paradise, and Cain and Abel.* Translated by John J. Savage. The Fathers of the Church 42. Washington, DC: The Catholic University of America Press, 1961.

Aquinas, Thomas. *Summa Theologiae.* Translated by Fr. Laurence Shapcote, OP. Edited by John Mortensen and Enrique Alarcón. Lander, WY: The Aquinas Institute for the Study of Sacred Doctrine, 2012.

Athanasius. *Select Works and Letters.* Nicene and Post-Nicene Fathers 4. Edited by Archibald Robertson. Peabody, MA: Hendrickson, 1994.

Athanasius the Great and Didymus the Blind. *Works on the Spirit.* Translated, with an Introduction and Annotations, by Mark DelCogliano, Andrew Radde-Gallwitz, and Lewis Ayres. Yonkers, NY: St. Vladimir's Seminary Press, 2011.

Augustine. *City of God.* Translated by Henry Bettenson. Harmondsworth, UK: Penguin, 1972.

———. *Confessions.* Translated by Henry Chadwick. Oxford: Oxford University Press, 1991.

———. *Confessions and Enchiridion.* Translated by Albert C. Outler. Philadelphia: Westminster, 1955.

———. *On Christian Doctrine.* Translated by D. W. Robertson Jr. New York: Liberal Arts Press, 1958.

Baptism, Eucharist, and Ministry. Faith and Order Paper No. 111. Geneva: World Council of Churches, 1982.

Barrett, C. K. *Acts: A Shorter Commentary.* London: T. & T. Clark, 2002.

Basil of Caesarea. *Exegetic Homilies.* Translated by Sister Agnes Clare Way, CDP. The Fathers of the Church 46. Washington, DC: The Catholic University of America Press, 1963.

Pope Benedict XVI (as Joseph Cardinal Ratzinger). *Introduction to Christianity.* San Francisco: Ignatius, 2004.

Pope Benedict XVI. *Jesus of Nazareth: From the Baptism in the Jordan to the Transfiguration.* Vol. 1. Translated by Adrian J. Walker. New York: Image, 2007.

———. *Jesus of Nazareth: Holy Week: From the Entrance into Jerusalem to the Resurrection.* Vol. 2. Translation provided by the Vatican Secretariat of State. San Francisco: Ignatius, 2011.

Bonaventure. *Bonaventure: The Soul's Journey into God, The Tree of Life, The Life of St. Francis.* Translated by Ewert Cousins. Mahwah, NJ: Paulist, 1978.

Calvin, John. *Institutes of the Christian Religion.* Translated by Henry Beveridge. Peabody, MA: Hendrickson, 2008.

Chambers, Nathan J. *Reconsidering Creation Ex Nihilo in Genesis 1.* Journal of Theological Interpretation Supplement 19. University Park, PA: Eisenbrauns, 2020.

Collins, Kenneth J., and Jason E. Vickers, eds. *The Sermons of John Wesley: A Collection for the Christian Journey.* Nashville: Abingdon, 2013.

Congar, Yves. *I Believe in the Holy Spirit: The Complete Three-Volume Work in One Volume.* Translated by David Smith. New York: Crossroad, 1983.

Daley, Brian E., SJ, ed. and trans. *Light on the Mountain: Greek Patristic and Byzantine Homilies on the Transfiguration of the Lord.* Yonkers, NY: St. Vladimir's Seminary Press, 2003.

Edwards, Jonathan. *The Sermons of Jonathan Edwards: A Reader.* Edited by Wilson H. Kimnach, Kenneth P. Minkema, and Douglas A. Sweeney. New Haven, CT: Yale University Press, 1999.

The Episcopal Church. *The Book of Common Prayer and Administration of the Sacraments and Other Rites and Ceremonies of the Church.* New York: Church Publishing Incorporated, 1979.

Gilbey, Monsignor A. N. *We Believe: A Simple Commentary on the Catechism of Christian Doctrine Approved by the Archbishops and Bishops of England and Wales.* Leominster, UK: Gracewing, 2011.

Gregory of Nazianzus. *On God and Christ: The Five Theological Orations and Two Letters to Cledonius.* Translated by Frederick Williams (Oration 27) and Lionel Wickham (Orations 28–31). Crestwood, NY: St. Vladimir's Seminary Press, 2002.

Gregory of Nyssa. *The Life of Moses.* Translated by Abraham J. Malherbe and Everett Ferguson. Mahwah, NJ: Paulist, 1978.

Hamilton, Victor P. *The Book of Genesis: Chapters 1–17.* The New International Commentary on the Old Testament. Grand Rapids: Eerdmans, 1990.

Hymns for Those That Seek and Those That Have Redemption in the Blood of Jesus Christ. London: Strahan, 1747. Accessed through the website of the Center for Studies in the Wesleyan Tradition, Duke Divinity School.

Irenaeus of Lyons. *Against the Heresies.* Translated and annotated by Dominic J. Unger, OFM CAP. Ancient Christian Writers 65. Mahwah, NJ: Newman, 2012.

Isaac the Syrian. *The Ascetical Homilies of St. Isaac the Syrian.* Translated by the Holy Transfiguration Monastery. Boston: Holy Transfiguration Monastery, 2011.

John of Damascus. *Writings.* The Fathers of the Church 37. Translated by Frederic H. Chase Jr. Washington, DC: The Catholic University of America Press, 1958.

John Paul II. *Rosarium Virginis Mariae.* Apostolic Letter. Vatican website. October 16, 2002. http://www.vatican.va/content/john-paul-ii/en/apost_letters/2002/documents/hf_jp-ii_apl_20021016_rosarium-virginis-mariae.html.

———. *Veritatis splendor.* Encyclical Letter. Vatican website. August 6, 1993. http://www.vatican.va/content/john-paul-ii/en/encyclicals/documents/hf_jp-ii_enc_06081993_veritatis-splendor.html.

Johnson, Junius. *The Father of Lights: A Theology of Beauty.* Grand Rapids: Baker Academic, 2020.

Johnson, Maxwell E. *The Rites of Christian Initiation: Their Evolution and Interpretation (Revised and Expanded Edition).* Collegeville, MN: Pueblo, 2007.

Jones, Beth Felker. *God the Spirit: Introducing Pneumatology in Wesleyan and Ecumenical Perspective*. Eugene, OR: Cascade, 2014.

Julian of Norwich. *Revelations of Divine Love*. Translated by Elizabeth Spearing. London: Penguin, 1998.

Koskela, Douglas M. "John Wesley." In *The Oxford Handbook of the Epistemology of Theology*, edited by William J. Abraham and Frederick D. Aquino, 459–70. Oxford: Oxford University Press, 2017.

Lossky, Vladimir. *In the Image and Likeness of God*. Crestwood, NY: St. Vladimir's Seminary Press, 1974.

MacKenzie, Iain M. *The "Obscurism" of Light: A Theological Study into the Nature of Light*. Norwich: Canterbury, 1996.

Maddox, Randy L., and Jason E. Vickers, eds. *The Cambridge Companion to John Wesley*. Cambridge: Cambridge University Press, 2010.

Nes, Solrunn. *The Uncreated Light: An Iconographical Study of the Transfiguration in the Eastern Church*. Grand Rapids: Eerdmans, 2007.

O'Collins, Gerald, SJ, and Mary Ann Meyers, eds. *Light from Light: Scientists and Theologians in Dialogue*. Grand Rapids: Eerdmans, 2012.

Pelikan, Jaroslav. *The Light of the World: A Basic Image in Early Christian Thought*. New York: Harper & Brothers, 1962.

Pinckaers, Servais, OP *The Pursuit of Happiness—God's Way: Living the Beatitudes*. Translated by Mary Thomas Noble, OP. Eugene, OR: Wipf & Stock, 1998.

Prestige, G. L. *God in Patristic Thought*. Eugene, OR: Wipf & Stock, 1964.

Pseudo-Dionysius. *Pseudo-Dionysius: The Complete Works*. Translated by Colm Luibheid. Mahwah, NJ: Paulist, 1987.

Pseudo-Macarius. *Pseudo-Macarius: The Fifty Spiritual Homilies and the Great Letter*. Translated by George A. Maloney, SJ. Mahwah, NJ: Paulist, 1992.

Ramsey, Arthur Michael. *The Glory of God and the Transfiguration of Christ*. London: Longmans, Green, and Co., 1949.

Rogers, Eugene F. Jr. *After the Spirit: A Constructive Pneumatology from Resources outside the Modern West*. Grand Rapids: Eerdmans, 2005.

Ruth, Lester. *A Little Heaven Below: Worship at Early Methodist Quarterly Meetings*. Nashville, TN: Kingswood, 2000.

Rutledge, Fleming. *Advent: The Once & Future Coming of Jesus Christ*. Grand Rapids: Eerdmans, 2018.

Satyavrata, Ivan. *The Holy Spirit: Lord and Life-Giver*. Carlisle, UK: Langham, 2012.

Schmemann, Alexander. *For the Life of the World: Sacraments and Orthodoxy*. Crestwood, NY: St. Vladimir's Seminary Press, 2004.

Symeon the New Theologian. *The Discourses*. Translated by C. J. deCatanzaro. Mahwah, NJ: Paulist, 1980.

———. *On the Mystical Life: The Ethical Discourses, Vol. 1: The Church and Last Things*. Translated by Alexander Golitzin. Crestwood, NY: St. Vladimir's Seminary Press, 1995.

———. *On the Mystical Life: The Ethical Discourses, Vol. 2: On Virtue and Christian Life*. Translated by Alexander Golitzin. Crestwood, NY: St. Vladimir's Seminary Press, 1996.

Teresa of Avila. *Interior Castle*. Translated and edited by E. Allison Peers. New York: Image, 1989.

Tozer, A. W. *The Knowledge of the Holy*. San Francisco: HarperOne, 1961.

Ware, Bishop Kallistos. *The Orthodox Way.* Revised Edition. Crestwood, NY: St. Vladimir's Seminary Press, 2001.

Wesley, John. *A Collection of Hymns for the Use of the People Called Methodists.* London: Paramore, 1780.

———. *Pocket Hymn Book.* London: Paramore, 1785. Accessed through the website of the Center for Studies in the Wesleyan Tradition, Duke Divinity School.

Wesley, John, and Charles Wesley. *Hymns and Sacred Poems.* London: Strahan, 1739. Accessed through the website of the Center for Studies in the Wesleyan Tradition, Duke Divinity School.

———. *Hymns and Sacred Poems.* London: Strahan, 1740. Accessed through the website of the Center for Studies in the Wesleyan Tradition, Duke Divinity School.

Williams, Rowan. *Tokens of Trust: An Introduction to Christian Belief.* Louisville, KY: Westminster John Knox, 2007.